From PRISON To Praise

Sonja G Vaughn

Unless noted otherwise, scripture quotation is forming New International King James Version of the Holy Bible.

Cover design by MT Graphics

Cover photo by Sylvia Dunnavant

Manufactured in the United States of America.

Library of Congress Data in Progress ISBN.

Acknowledgements

From Prison to Praise is dedicated to the memory of my loving mother, Hannah Marie Wallace! She pushed me to become God's best by any means necessary. Reminding me that when we take the "dis" out of disability, we can begin to shift our focus to the "ability" that remains, and that's what's important. My disabilities have enabled me to discover what my abilities really are. They've taught me a lot about character and determination. I want my undertakings to be examples to others that they too can accomplish whatever they set out to do.

First and foremost, I would like to thank God for creating me with purpose and potential in mind. He gave me the strength to endure all my struggles, life situations and circumstances and then allowed me to replace the bitterness of life with love, kindness and a forgiving heart.

Also, I would like to thank my best friend and confidant, Leonard Brown, for pushing me into my destiny, as well as our children, Divon and Sontoya Crutchfield; and Duan, Dewayne and Deon Brown, who continue to show me support and love by not making my past mistakes and failures blemishes but stepping stones.

Last, but certainly not least, thanks to Sylvia Dunnavant, Denise Marcia, Michael Tyree (MT Graphics), Kerry Malone (Mirror Image International) and Ryan Rattliff for their hard work to make sure *From Prison to Praise* was brought to life. Through your patience with me and your constant encouragement to keep pushing, I was able to complete this project in order to inspire the ones that struggle through life to keep striving and trusting God to take them from their Prison to their Praise.

FOREWORD
Elder Monte Lester
Cedar Grove Church

I feel very fortunate because I have had an opportunity to see snap shots of both the before and after pictures of Minister Sonja Vaughn Brown.

In my mind, I can still recall the very shy and innocent girl that I used to speak to as she passed by me in the hallways at high school. When I got to see her again, she had gone through a series of events and God had turned her life completely around.

Even though Murfreesboro is just a small town in Tennessee, I never got to see Minister Brown when she was incarcerated or any of the intricate parts of her testimony. But as I look at her minister now, it is a perfect picture of the amazing grace of God. I do believe that God is a God of change. And, I know that He is a God of second chances.

The Bible tells us that, "if a man be in Christ that he is a new creation and old things have passed away and all things are new."

Minister Sonja Brown's ministry *From Prison to Praise* is a prime example of God's love. I don't believe God judges us on our past but on our potential. She reminds me a lot of Apostle Peter. In Luke 22:32, Jesus speaks to Peter and says, "But I have prayed for you, that your faith should not fail; and when you have returned to *Me,* strengthen your brethren."

There were so many people that were trusting and believing that her conversion would come. It was their prayers that helped move her to ministry. After He brought her out, the Lord had placed a call on Minister Brown to go back and strengthen her "brother."

True ministry is about going back into the battlefield, to claim the lost and wounded. Minister Brown's ministry allows her to go into places that many people cannot or just will not go. She reaches in to help people like herself who have gotten caught up in the traps and entanglements of life.

Many lives have been changed because of what she has done. Minister Brown is a mighty weapon and angel in the Kingdom of God. Her book, *From Prison to Praise,* will just be another tool for her to help set the captive free.

After working with her in ministry, I know that she is as authentic as they come. God has truly changed her heart. He has used her to have authority with her Spirit filled testimony. She is a genuine, loving, kind and trustworthy person.

I am glad that I have had an opportunity to co-labor in ministry with her, and I look forward to the fruit that she will bare as her ministry continues to spread across the country.

Table of Contents

For I know the thoughts that I think toward you, saith the LORD, thoughts of peace, and not of evil, to give you an expected end."
Jeremiah 29:11 (KJV)

Chapter One

A Sinner's Prayer

It was about three o'clock on a misty morning in Murfreesboro, Tennessee. The date was August 4, 1997, a day that will forever be etched in my memory. I had experienced a long week of smoking crack, and every cell in my body was aching from exhaustion. I felt like I hadn't slept in days. All I kept saying to myself repeatedly was, *"I just need some rest."*

I had been chasing drugs for 12 years, and it had taken a toll on my mind, my body and my spirit.

Even though a part of me was afraid to get high because I had recently overdosed, there was still a much stronger tug within my soul to try to secure my next hit. For almost a decade, crack had captured the very essence of my being. It had manipulated me like a puppet on a string. As much as I wanted to separate myself, I could not break the ties that bound me.

Now, I was so weak that I could barely stand up by myself. My petite frame couldn't have weighed more than 80 pounds wringing wet with cement boots on. I struggled to walk down the street without falling over my own two feet. Yet, I kept moving because deep inside, I knew that I had to win this battle. Death was standing at my doorsteps; if I didn't beat drugs, they were going to drag me to my grave.

Like a lover, crack had crept into my heart and made me forget everything that should have mattered to me. I no longer cared about food, my family or shelter. Right now, I was coming down from a several-day drug binge; I needed another hit so bad that I could taste it.

As I stumbled down the road in the darkness, I looked for a place to sit down for a moment. The more I walked, the weaker I felt.

I was almost about to pass out when I saw the perfect spot on the corner of a curb by the end of a road. At this time of the morning, it was so quiet in Murfreesboro that you could almost hear a pin drop. The only noise for miles around was the sound of crickets and grasshoppers.

Sitting there in the middle of the openness, I began to reflect over my life. The first thing I wondered was how in the world I had allowed myself to get to this point? Precious moments in my life had evaporated in a puff of crack smoke; most of my adult life had become a blur because I was too busy trying to chase something that I would never catch.

Resting on that curb allowed me to do something that I hadn't done often: objectively analyze my circumstances and decisions. I got to thinking about what was going on in my life. Realizing all the bad choices that I had made over the last few years forced my emotions to the surface. Without warning, tears began to roll down my cheeks onto the cement ground surrounding me.

I tried to catch the water from my face, but my frail fingertips were no match for the well of emotion gushing from the depth of my soul.

The tears brought with them so many unanswered questions. What in the world had I done to myself? Would I ever be able to get out of this mess? Who in the world could trust me? But, the biggest question of them all was, who am I?

I was only 29 years old, and for almost ten years, I had been on a non-stop roller coaster of substance abuse. I desperately wanted to get off the ride, I just didn't know how.

I had been to jail so many times, most of the officers knew me by name. My rap sheet was so long that it looked like a well-written novel. I had stolen from everyone around town, except my family. Yet, my family didn't want anything to do with me. I was a Prisoner in my own body. I was considered a menace to society. I hurt everyone around me, including myself.

With the stars above me and bugs buzzing all around me, I thought about throwing a pity party. Yet, I would be the only invited guest and I didn't even have the strength to blow out the candle on my pity-cake. This was going to have to be my "come-to-Jesus" meeting. I might never get another chance.

Although I couldn't piece things together to find out how I had gotten myself in this position, I knew if I was going to survive, I had to change. My thousand-dollar-a-day drug habit was holding me hostage like a thief in the night. I didn't have a job or any other means to support myself. This meant I had committed every crime you could imagine and some that you couldn't just to support my addiction.

But somehow in the middle of this dirt road, I was coming to grips with myself. I knew there was no way that I could continue this path. It was a road of self-destruction and pain. I couldn't continue like this much longer.

With tears rolling down my face, I cried out to God. I had heard that God didn't answer sinners' prayers, but my life depended on Him answering this one.

As my hands shook in front of my face, I said, "God I would rather die than stay like this."

Even though I had been in and out of jail over 30 times, I begged God to let me go back to jail one more time. "God the next time that I go to jail, you keep me until you know that I will do right when I get out," I pleaded. Using what little strength that I had left, I continued to barter with God. Deep in my spirit, I knew that jail represented stability and structure for me. I used to make sure that I got caught when I got tired and needed a place to rest my head. I was tired, and jail was a haven for me.

My lifestyle was catching up with me. I knew that I couldn't continue down the journey I was on much longer. A dead-end crash was inevitable, and I was begging for an intervention from Jesus before it happened.

Just as I let out my last plea to God, I felt a hand on my shoulder. When I raised my head, I could see the frame of an older woman out of the corner of my eye. Based on her white hair and wrinkled skin, I knew that she had to be in her late 70's. Once she knew that she had my attention, she said, "Baby, don't cry. God has something for you to do."

All I could think was that was easy for her to say. I knew there was no way that she could even begin to comprehend my situation. Still determined to feel sorry for myself, I buried my head deep into palms of my hands and continued to cry. "You just don't understand," I said.

Still weeping, I told her once more, "You just don't understand." Then I turned my head toward her voice. To my surprise there was no longer anyone one standing by me. I was all alone.

I turned to look across the street, and there was still no one there. I stood up and looked down the street, but I still didn't see anyone. Although it was dark outside, the area was wide open. It would take a long time for someone to get far away enough to be out of sight. By her touch, and the sound of her voice, this lady was much too old to have gotten away that fast. It was impossible for her to have been out of sight without a trace in minutes.

I sat back down on the curb side and tried to gather my thoughts one more time. This chain of events had startled me. I had no logical way of describing the woman's presence and then disappearance into thin air. This entire scene just took me back to Sunday school when I was a little girl. I remember one of the teachers saying, "Be careful how you entertain strangers, because you may very well be entertaining angels."

Looking around at the dark vacant streets, I realized I had my answer. This woman must have been an angel! God had sent an angel to let me know that He could still hear the prayers of a sinner. Somewhere in my soul, I knew that He cared enough about me to send me a message in the midnight hour of my life, during my messy situation.

After all, I realized that the Lord had been protecting me while I was entangled in the street. His distinct guidance kept me out of danger. There would be times that I would feel this urgency to leave the scene, and I would find out that something crazy happened after I left. As much as I liked to get high, there were times that I would refuse drugs. I just knew that there was something wrong with them. It would be later revealed that batch was laced with something that was deadly.

Other times, there would be something in my gut that would warn me before there was going to be a shooting where I was. I would hear about it later. Even though I couldn't keep up with much of anything, God was keeping up with me.

I spent the rest of the night reflecting on what the lady had said, and how God had always been there for me. I had no idea how He was going to use me or what was going to happen next. A few days later the mystery would unfold. On August 8, 1997, I would get the much-needed rest that I had been longing for. For the thirty-second time since I had been addicted to crack, I would go to jail.

But this time would be different. A routine arrest for forgery, which should have resulted in a few weeks of jail, turned into nearly three years in prison. When my luck ran out, God stepped in. I would never again have to wonder if God answered the prayers of those that were not saved. That summer night He reached into the pits of hell and pulled me out. He sent an angel so that I could wrestle with death.

I am a living witness that God answers sinners' prayers. He heard my midnight cry and sent an angel to give me a word that would lead me from the wilderness of his destruction to His purpose for my life. Even though I went to prison, the Lord gave me a praise from the depth of his heart. I have been praising Him ever since.

"My lips shall greatly rejoice when I sing unto thee; and my soul, which thou hast redeemed." Psalm 71:23 (KJV)

Chapter Two

Selected to be Unique

When I was a little girl, it was obvious to my family that I was going to be a little different. My mom said that when I was born, she knew that I was "either possessed by the devil or touched by angels."

My early development would be a sign of my uniqueness. My aunts and cousins still tease me because they say I used to remind them of a robot. Everywhere I went, I would crawl in slow motion. When someone called my name, it would take me "all day" to turn to them.

My mom said that I would be on the other side of the room and she'd call out to me, "Candy, come here." She would watch me take the long journey toward her in a very slow and methodical motion. She never said another word, she just watched me move toward her. When she told this story to me and to the family, she recalled it with great laughter. "I thought it was going to take her all day," she laughed. By the time I finally made it to her, she would shake her head wondering what in the world I would do next.

Not long after that episode, she said, "One day, you took your time and pulled yourself up to your feet holding onto one end of the table. Once you got your balance, you stood there for a few minutes and looked around the room. The next thing I knew you turned around and took off running." The family's biggest question was, how do you go from barely being able to crawl to running in just a matter of minutes?

These early relocations of my life would be indicative of what was to come. My mother loved telling people how I never learned to walk, that instead I just started running. I guess I have been running ever since. When my mother would remind me of this story, she would always have a warning attached to it. "Candy, just make sure you are running *to* something and not *from* something."

During my early childhood years, I wasn't concerned about running from anything, because I was surrounded by a lot of love.

I had one brother and 3 sisters – I was next to the youngest – so there was usually a lot going on in our household.

To top it off, my dad had plenty of outside children. It seemed like every time you turned around some woman was dropping off her child at our front doorstep saying to my mama, "This is your husband's baby." For most women those might have been fighting words, but for mama it was just another person in our house to love. She would grab the kid by the hand and open her heart to the new addition to our family.

Many times, I felt like she treated the outside children better than she did us. I think she might have been trying to overcompensate for a bad situation. But if anyone asked her about it, she always said, "It isn't the child fault, they didn't ask to be here." Then she would add, "We don't want them to feel like an outsider."

After a while there were more of them than there was us. I really didn't care if they felt like an outsider or not. I just knew that my dad needed to stop having outside babies, because this was too much for everyone to bare.

Although I always desired to be close to my father, my strongest relationship was with my mother. My mother was like my best friend.

When we were alone, she would even confess to me, "You are my favorite." I made the mistake of sharing that with my siblings one day, which started a small rift between all of us. My mother had to counteract my claim by saying that we were all her favorites. Of course, that made me feel a little less special, but this kept peace in the household.

Instead of there being confusion between us, my mother really wanted me to celebrate my difference. She used to say, "You trying to fit in with your brothers and sisters and you not supposed to fit in. You are supposed to just be you."

For me, getting along with my brothers and sisters was like trying to fit a square peg into a round whole. It was possible, but it would take a lot of work.

The Wrong Touch

To ease the tension with my siblings, my mother decided to let me go stay with my grandmother's sister. She was my great aunt, but everyone simply called her Sis. Aunt Sis didn't have any children. She and my Uncle Johnny were always keeping somebody's kids. They were well off and they loved to share their blessed lifestyle with everyone. They seemed to enjoy hosting children of various family members.

I wasn't too disappointed about this decision, because I knew that they would go out of their way to make me comfortable. At first going to stay with them was like a dream come true.

Aunt Sis reminded me of Aunt Esther on the sitcom *Sanford and Son*. She had a deep brown completion with a wide, toothy grin. She was a little bit on the slim side, and boy could she cook! On the other hand, her husband Johnny was short, with a receding hairline. He sorts of strutted when he walked like George Jefferson from the television show *The Jefferson's*. When I first went to stay with them, it felt like their main objective in life was to spoil me rotten.

When I was with them, I felt like a princess. I had my own room and my own television. It was wonderful not having to share anything. With four siblings, that was almost unheard of at home. They even made a point to take me shopping when I first got there. They bought clothes, toys and all kinds of things to fix up my room.

Although I was only seven years old, all the things they gave me made me feel as if I had everything that I'd ever need in life. I almost wanted someone to pinch me so that I knew that I wasn't dreaming.

Then one night my dream turned into a nightmare. My aunt had just come in and turned off the television in my room. She kissed me on the forehead and said, "Candy, you better go to sleep, or you won't want to get up in the morning."

Scooting under the covers, I replied, "Yes ma'am."

Before long I was fast asleep. Soon, I was awakened by someone pulling at my night clothes. Before I could say anything, a hand went over my mouth. My uncle Johnny said, "Shhhh, be quiet, we don't want to wake up Sis."

I was still sleepy, and I could not understand what was going on. Why did he want to make sure my aunt didn't wake up? What was my uncle doing in my room this late anyway? Why was he putting his hand under my night clothes? Nobody had done that before.

It didn't take long for me to get an answer to my questions. The next thing I knew I felt his other hand going between my legs. I didn't know why he was doing this. Somehow, I knew this had to be wrong, but there was nothing that I could do to stop him. I was helpless.

All sudden, I started feeling these weird sensations in my body that I didn't understand as a young girl. I didn't know what was going on. Tears began to roll down my face and onto my pillow. He continued to fondle me until he got tired. He told me, "This is going to be our little secret. You must not tell your auntie."

I didn't respond. By this time my pillow was soaking wet from my tears. I guess he wasn't certain that he could trust my silence because before he closed my bedroom door he said, "If you tell your aunt, I'll hurt your mother." It was impossible for me to go to sleep that night. My world had changed in just a few minutes. At least at home, I had my siblings to share things with, now I was all alone.

The next day, I followed his instructions. I didn't say anything to my aunt. I thought that she would be able to tell that something was wrong – she never did.

After about six months this became "our" secret routine. My aunt would go to bed. I would be in my room. The next thing I knew I would have a "visitor."

I wasn't the average child, so I started thinking about what I could do to stop him from hurting me. If it was okay for Uncle Johnny to come in my room at night, why *couldn't* we tell Aunt Sis? He knew that I was crazy about my mama, why in the world would he threaten to hurt her?

One day I was sitting alone trying to make sense of all this, but I couldn't. It became evident to me that I needed to help myself.

At that point, I knew that I needed to devise a plan to stop my uncle. I guess while I was thinking I got quiet. My aunt said, "Baby what's wrong? You don't seem like yourself."

Trying not to give myself away, I responded, "I'm okay."

I kept thinking how she doesn't realize that something is going on. Why can't she protect me from my uncle? Doesn't she feel him slipping out of bed at night? Doesn't she realize that I am acting different?

It bothered me that at seven years old I had to protect myself. Even as a child, I was always the type of person that tried to take care of things myself because I didn't want to bother anyone else.

I didn't want to worry my mom, and I didn't want to hurt my aunt because she had been so nice to me. I concluded that this was something that I was going to have to resolve myself. That night I went to bed as usual, but I was determined that I was not going to be the victim anymore.

Just like always my uncle waited for my aunt to fall asleep. After I heard the television go off in her room, I heard my bedroom doorknob twist. I tried to lay as still as possible and pretend that I was asleep.

Suddenly, I felt the cover being pulled off me. Uncle Johnny reached down to pull my pajama bottoms down. I had taken the scissors out of my aunt's sewing chest. I held them tight in my right hand. As he tugged on my pajama bottoms, I pulled back my arm, and jabbed the scissors into his hand. He jumped up and let out a loud scream. I put my finger to my lips and went, "Shhhh, you don't want to wake up Aunt Sis."

I don't remember what he said but he was cursing up a storm as he ran out the door with blood dripping from his hand. How in the world my aunt slept through all that commotion, I don't know? Maybe the same way she slept through him coming into my room night after night.

That night, I learned how to fend for myself to keep my Uncle Johnny off me. This was just the beginning of me learning how to take care of myself. The experience would teach me that many of life's lessons don't come with instructions. I had to learn that even when I didn't know what to do that God would be with me.

Even though I was young, I realized that I could not let this violation hold me back. Fortunately, I never thought that any of this was my fault. I knew that I was not responsible for my aunt not paying attention to what was going on in her own household. I never thought it was my fault that my mother never noticed my demeanor change.

I would later learn that when there is a molester in the family, there is usually more than one person being affected. My aunt and uncle were always taking in kids. It would be much later that other stories would emerge. What is done in the dark always comes to light, it just a matter of time.

God uniquely developed my character through these incidents. He helped me realize this violation of my young, underdeveloped body would strengthen my knowledge about what I could and could not control.

"I will bless the LORD at all times: his praise shall continually be in my mouth. My soul shall make her boast in the LORD: the humble shall hear thereof and be glad. O magnify the LORD with me and let us exalt his name together." Psalm 34:1-3 (KJV)

Chapter Three

Dancing without Daddy

My molestation would not just end with my uncle. One Christmas, I was in a major department store and the manager was dressed up as Santa. He said, "Little girl, come sit right here on my lap."

When I did, he slipped his hands under my dress and tried to fondle me. I felt him tugging at my panties, I jumped up off his lap and ran to security. I had learned my lesson from my past experiences with my uncle, and I wasn't going to keep any more secrets.

Even though the experience in the store was nothing like my encounters with my uncle, this began to cause major trust issues with men. I didn't know what they would do to me if I was alone with them.

By the time I was thirteen, I had experienced more in my life than most children my age. Yet, there was still a part of me that longed to be like any other girl. I wanted to play with dolls and ride my bike. Then one day everything around me crumbled like a sandcastle in the rain.

The one part of my life that I thought was stable was my home life. I just felt like my mother and father were my rocks; I knew they would always be there for me. Yet, without any notice at all, my entire household went through a major overhaul.

After years of infidelity, my mother decided that she could no longer take it. With the flip of a pen she divorced my daddy. My life was shattered. They had been married twenty-six years. This just didn't make sense to my adolescent mind.

I was a pre-teen going through hormonal and physical changes compounded with the additional emotional turmoil of dealing with my mom leaving my dad. I wasn't old enough to understand the financial ramifications of her having to take care of my brother, my younger sister, and myself. I just knew that things were going to change. I didn't have a clue how drastic that change would be.

At first, trying to get used to life without my dad was hard. I was angry at my mother. My father's infidelity was nothing new to anyone. It seemed like when he had finally stopped whoring around, she decided to leave him. I just couldn't wrap my mind around the motivation behind her decision. But then again, I was only 13.

I wasn't old enough to realize that while my mother was welcoming baby after baby in our household from my father's extra marital affairs, she had already checked out of the marriage. Although the divorce was new for my siblings and me, it was evident that she had made her final decision years before the ink had dried on the divorce papers.

The thing that made the situation more stressful for me to deal with was that a year after my mother left my dad — she remarried. I hadn't gotten over my dad being away, and she moved someone else in to take his place.

With the addition of a new man to the household, my anger turned to bitterness. It took everything in me to welcome my stepfather, James, in the house.

By the time my mother married James, we had fallen on hard times. We were all crammed into a small trailer home. Things had gotten just that bad.

James, who people in the community called Skeebo, was a short and stocky guy, who only stood about 5'3. He didn't seem that threatening to us, because he wasn't that big. He had sort of a non-assuming presence. You wouldn't run from him, even if you saw him in a dark alley at night. Yet, he had this hypnotizing power over my mother.

After they got married, he helped her open a bootleg liquor joint so that she could sell liquor on the side to make extra money. Once the joint opened it seemed like my mother was drunk all the time – if she wasn't selling liquor, she was drinking it.

I don't know if she was drinking in order to forget how bad things were, or if she was drinking to fit in with the customers of her bootleg joint. All I knew was that she and James were either drinking, fighting, or having sex. Sometimes it seemed like all the above.

One day they got into fight, butt-naked right in the middle of house. My brother and I jumped in to try to break it up. It was so embarrassing, because I didn't want my brother to see mama like this, and he didn't want me to see James. The funniest thing was that neither of them seemed to care who saw them. They were cussing, throwing things, and their private parts were very public.

With James around, there always seemed to be an air of sexuality. Sometimes there was so much sex around, that it made me uncomfortable. One day I had to get milk money for school from James. I walked in their bedroom unannounced and he was watching an X-rated movie. His shirt was off, and his jeans were unbuttoned. The people on the television were going at it like dogs in heat. All I could hear was moaning and groaning.

When I first walked in the room, I looked at the television screen, and then I looked away. I couldn't believe what I was seeing. I waited for him to stop the movie, but he acted like there was nothing wrong. He just reached in his pocket and pulled out his wallet. Not even looking me in the face, he stuck out his hand with the money in it and said, "Here you go." As I walked out the door with my eyes big as baseballs in total disbelief, he continued to watch the movie.

I couldn't believe it; I was a 14-year-old young lady and he didn't even have enough respect for me or himself to stop watching an X- rated movie in my presence. What kind of man was he? To top it off I couldn't take two steps inside their bedroom without stepping on a porn magazine. There were pictures of boobs and body parts everywhere I stepped. There was so much porn paraphernalia in their bedroom it looked like an adult bookstore.

With the sexual doors that had been opened to me by my uncle, being around James made me feel very uncomfortable. He never tried anything with me, but I just didn't trust him. It seemed like he was obsessed with sex. I knew that my dad didn't pay that much attention to my mother, but I couldn't understand how she went from getting so little affection to becoming a "sex freak."

Based on my limited assessment of the situation, my mother had gone from one extreme to the other. She had gone from someone that didn't pay her much attention, to someone that was all over her. Both cases were extreme. I didn't know how to change things for my mother, but I knew I had to change some things for myself.

"**But** ye are a chosen generation, a royal priesthood, a holy nation, a peculiar people; that ye should shew forth the praises of him who hath called you out of darkness into his marvelous light." *I Peter 2:9 (KJV)*

Chapter Four

A Date with Danny

After a year of listening to James and my mother fighting all the time, and endless exposure to all kinds of sexual innuendos – I knew it was time to move on. I just didn't know what I was going to do, or where I was going to go.

Then one day I was visiting my grandmother, and I met this boy that was hanging out in the neighborhood. His sister lived next door, and she thought it would be a good idea for us to meet. He was a book worm and didn't have a lot of friends.

When I first saw him, I thought he was sort of cute. He had light skin and was a little on the thin side. He had a smooth, warm, almond-colored complexion, and deep, penetrating brown eyes.

Even though he was very shy, we seemed to connect. I don't know how we started talking but before I knew it, we were carrying on a great conversation. After a while it felt like we had known each other for years. His name was Danny Crutchfield.

The first day that we met, Danny and I hung out all day at my grandmother's house. When he left, my grandmother had a twinkle in her eye. Looking at me with this big smile on her face, she said, "You sure do know how to pick them, don't you?" I was blushing, because I knew that her comment had something to do with Danny.

Putting my hands on my hips coyly, I continued to joke with my grandmother, "Now you know that he wanted to meet me."

My grandmother just kept on teasing me, "Don't be shy now. You weren't shy when young Mr. Crutchfield was around here." She paused and added, "His family got plenty of money. You better believe his sister is going to be watching every step that you take."

Although I heard what my grandmother was saying. It really didn't register with me. Before long, Danny and I started spending more time together. Then he started buying me stuff. At first the gifts were small, then they kept getting bigger and bigger.

I never had anybody buy me stuff like that before, so I began to equate love with money. The more he bought, the more that I thought he loved me. After we had been talking for about 6 months, he bought me a Ford Granada. I just knew that he was the one! I was a junior in high school and almost nobody had a car. You couldn't tell me that I wasn't hot stuff.

The car was the prelude to Danny's popping the question of marriage. I was barely 16 when he asked me to marry him. When he proposed, I felt like my heart left my body and was dancing with the stars. It was the happiest day of my life. I jumped off the porch, straight into his arms. He held me tight as he kissed my forehead. I knew that our love was going to last forever.

We had one small detail to deal with; I was going to have to convince my father to sign the papers for me to get married. In the state of Tennessee, you must be 18 years old to get married, and by our wedding date I was only 16.

It took a lot of convincing for my father to agree, but he finally decided to sign the consent papers giving Danny and me permission to become husband and wife.

Danny was three years older than I was. His parents had set him up in his own computer company, so he was able to pay for our entire wedding all by himself. In those days $15,000 for a wedding was a lot of money.

Our wedding was considered a high society wedding. Many of the prominent people from Murfreesboro and Nashville came out to see me wed young Mr. Crutchfield. I am sure there were several girls that had their eyes on his wallet, but his heart belonged to me.

Although this had to be the biggest moment of my life, the day I got married I felt like a little girl who had stumbled into a fairytale. Our wedding was huge. I had 7 bridesmaids, 7 groomsmen, and a maid of honor, a best man, a ring bearer and a flower girl. The minister, who was extremely tall, towered over us as we recited our vows.

It probably looked like a mock wedding with us kids just playing dress up. To make things worse when we got up to the pulpit, we seemed so small. The minister was standing several feet above us. I can still hear him say, "I now pronounce you Mr. and Mrs. Danny Ray Crutchfield."

As we turned around to face all our warm-hearted friends, I felt like my life was just about to begin. I was ready to put all the horrible events of my past behind me and step into a new world full of possibilities.

Danny's parents ran a large construction company. They decided as a wedding gift to us, they would offer us the property right next door to their house. Little did I realize that my welcome mat would be next door to my in-laws.

Living next door to Danny's parents quickly turned from a blessing to a curse. We were young and didn't have an opportunity to get to know each other well. We were forced to contend with his family.

Before we got to know each other well as husband and wife, I realized I had to compete with his mother for Danny's attention. After work, he started going home to his mother before he came home to me.

Early on I began to resent his strong family ties. Instead of being greeted after work with hugs and kisses. I would hear comments like, "Mama doesn't look like that, or, daddy said we need to do this."

I was young and feisty, that I would have a quick come back, "Well, I isn't your mama, and Lord knows that I'm sure not trying to be your daddy."

Those words would be the beginning of our fighting, but soon enough we would make up.

Our first year was trying to say the least. I miscarried my first baby. I got pregnant again and lost that child as well. After the second baby died, the doctors sat us down and talked with us. They informed us that it didn't look like I was going to be able to carry a child to full term. I was crushed, but the doctor's words didn't seem to faze Danny at all.

I felt like not being able to have a baby was only compounding the problems of our marriage. I had married the youngest of 8 children, and it was becoming quite clear that I was just not good enough. I was saved, sanctified and filled with the Holy Ghost. I just didn't' fit in. Yet, no one had figured this out before we got married.

One day, Danny and I were next door visiting his parents. They had a very modern custom-made, split-level home. The kitchen was upstairs, and the den was downstairs. His mom and I were sitting downstairs in the den, and Danny and his father were in the kitchen talking. Then Danny yelled down at me," Sonja, will you bring us some water?"

I just looked at his mom, because I knew he couldn't be serious – he was right there!

Pulling her chair back, she said, "The glasses are up at the top of the cabinet."

Now, I knew they were all crazy. I swung my chair around and cussing. "It will be a cold day in hell, before I get you some water." I couldn't believe that they were yelling down to me and they were sitting next to the refrigerator and the faucet.

Mrs. Crutchfield just looked at me like I had five heads, because she was a firm believer in doing what the man said.

Before Danny's mother had a chance to say anything, I heard his dad yell at Danny, "That is why you shouldn't have married her, she isn't' trained right."

Those were fighting words. I flew up the steps cussing out loud. I let his dad know that I wasn't scared of him, I said, "I am not no puppy, I don't need to be trained." At that, I was through – I went and finished watching my soaps!

All hell had broken out between mama and James. Things had gone from bad to worse between them.

Danny and I were sitting at home when the phone rang. Sometimes, I think I can smell trouble before it comes. I just knew that something was wrong with my mother. He never even gave me the phone. He just said, "Baby we got to go to the hospital."

"Danny don't tell me that something is wrong with my mama," I said trying to evade what I was feeling in my heart. Tears began to roll down my face, before I even got the news. I just knew it was bad. As always, my instinct was right.

James had stabbed my mother in the chest twice with a butcher block knife that left two holes in her heart. The only reason she survived was because she was so drunk that her body didn't realize that she had been stabbed.

As the family sat around the waiting room of the hospital, I kept getting bits and pieces of what had happened. My sister told me that after the stabbing, my mother ran down the street to get away from James, but she was too weak to get very far and - She passed. She told me that James just tossed her body in the back of his company car.

He pulled up to the circular driveway of the emergency room entrance and laid her body at the door. He didn't even wait for anyone to come out, he just took off, leaving her bleeding all over the place. I guess he was afraid that he was going to go to jail.

Once we found out that mama was going to be okay, my dad rounded everybody up and asked us to get in his car. Dad was a pretty mild-mannered guy; I had never seen him like this. His eyes were blood shot red. While everyone got into the car, he didn't even wait for the door to close, before he sped off toward James's house.

"If I can just get my hands on him, I'll kill him," he kept saying over and over with great conviction in his voice. Although mama and daddy hadn't been together in years, he still loved her.

I could feel every bump in the road as we sped toward James' house. When we pulled up in front of the house, we all jumped out and headed to the front door. My father banged on the door so hard, I am sure James thought we were the police.

When James came to the door, we pushed our way inside. Then my sister pulled out a gun and pointed it at James. Throwing a quick jab to his chest, my dad said, "If you ever lay another hand on my wife, you will not live to tell about it," I couldn't believe how valiant my father had been. But I still had to correct him. "Daddy that's not your wife, she's his wife."

By this time my dad had hit James so many times, he looked like an old, used punching bag. "I don't care whose wife she is. He better keeps his filthy hands off her." My dad whipped James like he had stolen something. Before things could get out of control, we pulled daddy off James. I said, "Daddy, it isn't worth you take his life. You got him good enough." I know that James was afraid to hit my father back, and there was no way that he was going to call the police. He was already scared that he was going to jail.

We all went back, and I stayed at the hospital all night long. I knew that I was blessed that my mother was still alive. The doctors had told us that during her operation they had lost her, but they were able to bring her back. I knew that God was giving my mother a second chance at life.

When mama finally woke up, I was sitting by her side. I know she could tell that I had been crying most of the night. She told me that she had an out-of-body experience and she could see everything that was going on.

Squeezing my hand, she said, "Sonja, I am not going nowhere." She paused and added, "I promise that I will let you know before I check out of here."

Once she was released from the hospital, she went straight back to James. I couldn't believe it. He had tried to kill her and now she was back with him. This was crazy. I just had to resolve in my head, whatever made her happy.

I later found out that mama had returned to James as a woman on a mission. Once they had made up and had sex, she let him go to sleep. Then she put a gun to his head, and said, "If you ever lay another hand on me, I'll kill you." The next day, James got up went to work and never came back.

After James left, my mama set out to get her life back on track. A few months later I would find out that I was pregnant again. This time I would carry the baby full term. I would finally get to be a mother, but my marriage was about to take a fatal blow.

"The LORD is my strength and song, and he is become my salvation: he is my God, and I will prepare him a habitation; my father's God, and I will exalt him." *Exodus 15:2 (KJV)*

Chapter Five

My Heart Belongs to Little D

My third pregnancy was a miracle. After having two miscarriages, I was not expecting to carry full term. I did all the wrong things: played football, went horseback riding, and ate whatever I wanted to eat. I acted like I wasn't pregnant, and surprise, this one stuck.

Life was finally being good to me. There was no joy that could compare with the elation I experienced from being a mother. The birth of our first son, Danny Crutchfield, Jr., whom we affectionately called Little D. was much more than my husband and I could ever express. Little D was not only our pride and joy, he was also the apple of his grandparents' eye. He bounced from our house to their house next door like a basketball on a court.

The birth of our first child was like the icing on the cake for our marriage. As a mother, I began to feel like I finally fit in. All my life I had felt like an ugly duckling. My sisters were always the ones getting the compliments on how pretty they were and how nice they looked. When it came to looks, I felt like it was them and then somewhere off in a distance there was me. Now with a man who loved me, and a son, it seemed like I had arrived.

After the birth of Little D, my focus was just being a good wife, good mother and a good business partner. I loved up on Danny, made his lunch and helped keep his books for his construction company. I even did household choirs. I was a little lazy with it, but I got it done. Sometimes getting it done meant hiring a maid. If I was washing a pot and it got burned, it was just time to buy a new pot. I was not going to put in the extra effort to try to clean it. Since we had the money, I just replaced it.

Overall, we didn't have any problems, accept my temper. I had the attitude that it was my way or the highway. I had a short fuse and it seemed like it was always being blown by someone. Sometimes it was Danny, sometimes it was my in-laws and sometimes it was my family. In fact, my temperament drove my in-laws crazy because they were trying to train me, and according to them I was untrainable.

At first trying to manage everything got to be a little overbearing. I knew that I needed help with Little D, so I started getting my little sister and some of her friends to help.

They were all about 13 at the time and living in the inner city. I felt like picking them up to help with the baby was as good for them as it was for me. I wanted them to see a different world. I didn't want my little sister Peaches to have to live the life I lived. I treated her and her friends to the finer things of life that I hadn't been accustomed to having. We lived in the country, so I took them horseback riding, shopping and eating out. When they were at my house, they had the run of the entire house. We never had money growing up, so I felt like the least I could do was to allow them to experience what it was like not to have to worry about finances. I also paid them well for babysitting my pride and joy.

Sometimes I would end up with about five girls for the weekend. They spent the night, spring breaks and during the summer they stayed for weeks at a time. They were full of life and energy and Danny and I enjoyed having them around. When I couldn't get the group of them, I would just get Peaches and her friend, Remand to help me.

There were times that my sister was busy, so I just started picking up Remanda to help. After a while Remanda became one of my regular babysitters. I knew that she understood the rules of my house, and I felt comfortable leaving her there when I had to do something. One weekend Remanda had been staying with us, and I decided to go get some groceries. I yelled in the back to Danny, "Hey honey, I am going to make a run. I'm leaving Remanda with Little D."

Before I could put my hands on the doorknob, Danny yelled back, "Sonja, you need to take Remanda with you. I'll look after Little D myself."

I just laughed and said, "You know that you can handle that little girl." Then I headed out the door and I didn't think a thing about it.

A few weeks later, Danny began to complain about Remanda jumping up and down on his lap. He said, "Sonja, you need to take that girl with you when you leave. Every time you're gone, she starts jumping on my lap and climbing on me."

I just thought that he was tripping. "Danny, she's just a kid. She hasn't been around a lot of love, so she just wants some attention," I said. I knew Danny was making a mountain out of mole hill. This little girl didn't mean him any harm. She was just a kid with a lot of energy.

This pattern continued for a while. Remanda would come over and I would leave. I knew that she had everything under control. Danny continued to complain, but I knew that he would get over it. After a while he stopped asking me to take her with me, and I knew that he had finally made the adjustment.

After Little D turned one, I started to feel there was something wrong in our marriage. I couldn't put my finger on it. Instead of trying to figure it out, I decided to start hanging out with my friends. I got this "wild hair" in my spirit. I thought that Danny was too country, so I began to go clubbing. I would pick up my sister and Remanda. We would go skating and sometimes shopping for most of the day. Then I would leave them at the house, so I could hit the clubs.

This became my regular routine for a while. My clubbing only added fuel to the fire for my in-laws. Danny's father would say things like: *While you at home with the baby, she's out at the clubs. What's wrong with that picture?* Although he was right, his father began to plant seeds of discord in our marriage. Eventually the seeds began to grow like a wildflower.

One night, I was at the club and this older lady walked up to me with a cane in her hand. She was slow but deliberate with her steps. When she got right in front of me, she stopped and asked, "Are you Mrs. Crutchfield?"

I had no idea why she wanted to know, so I just responded "Yes."

I wasn't the least bit concerned, because the woman looked like somebody's grandmother. She shouldn't have even been in the club.

Once she heard my response. She took one step back, to get her footing. She raised her cane like she was going to swing at me. I jumped back as an automatic reaction. I couldn't believe this woman was trying to hit me. By then all my friends had surrounded her.

"Lady, what in the world is wrong with you?" I asked as I tried to make sense of this situation.

Her eyes squinted with anger, she said, "You're asking what is wrong with me? I should beat the mess out of you. Your husband has gotten my grandbaby pregnant?"

"My husband has gotten your granddaughter pregnant. What in the world are you talking about? My husband is Danny Crutchfield, and he isn't got nobody pregnant!"

"My granddaughter is Remanda, and he has gotten her pregnant."

When she said Remanda, I fell back like somebody had shot me. I put my hand over my chest, "Your granddaughter is Remanda?"

"Yes, my granddaughter is Remanda and our family is sick; that girl is only 13-years-old! She is just a baby herself; she is too young to be having a baby. "

All my friends stepped back from the woman. They knew that Remanda was my babysitter. I couldn't even stand up anymore. The wind has been knocked out of me like I had been punched by Muhammad Ali. Still holding my chest, I staggered to the nearest seat.

I got in my car, and put the key in the ignition, and that is all I remembered. Everything from that point was a complete blur. Remanda, pregnant? Remanda pregnant by Danny? No, way. I tried to convince myself that this was not possible. This little girl could not be pregnant by my husband.

As I was turning onto our street, I flashed back. I could hear Danny saying: *Sonja, you need to take that girl with you; stop her from jumping up and down on my lap.*

What was wrong with me?! Why couldn't I see it before? Remanda wasn't built like a regular thirteen-year-old girl. She had the body of a grown woman. She was busty and shapely. In fact, her breasts were bigger than mine. Then I remembered, she wanted to come over, even when I didn't need her to babysit. By then, I felt like she was family. It really didn't matter to me if she was around when I wasn't home.

Instead of pulling into our driveway, I pulled into my in-law's driveway next door. I needed to find out what was going on. There was only one person who could answer the questions on my mind, and that was Mr. Danny Crutchfield himself.

I knocked on my in-law's door so hard I felt like my fist was going to go through the wood. I knew that Danny had to know that something was wrong, but he still opened the door.

With a bit of an attitude, he said, "Girl what's wrong with you? Little D just fell asleep."

"Well I guess you better wake him up," I said as I pushed the door open.

I couldn't wait to confront him with the news. I continued, "How can you fix your face to ask what is wrong with me? You got Remanda pregnant, and you have the nerve to ask what's wrong with me?"

"Sonja, you have lost your mind. What are you talking about?"

"Don't try to act like you don't know what I am talking about. This old lady tried to beat the crap out of me in the club tonight because she said you got her grandbaby pregnant. Danny, don't tell me that you done got that little girl pregnant."

"Well, you were never here. You were always going to the club, or hanging with your friends," he tried to justify his actions.

He could have said anything, but I was *never there*. I wanted him to tell me the lady wasn't telling the truth. I wanted this to be big mistake. His words let me know it was true. I just balled up my fist and hit him in the chest as hard as I could.

He raised his hands to push me back, his father walked in the room with a shot gun in his hand. "If you don't get off my property, I am going to blow your head off," he said pointing the gun in my direction. Of course, I left.

Walking to my car, tears were rolling down my face, all I could think was that I didn't see this coming. The little girl that I had befriended and tried to expose to the finer things of life had just blindsided me. She had wiggled her way into my heart and seduced my husband. My world was about to be shattered like a crystal glass. I never saw this coming.

Danny waited until the next day to come home with Little D; he knew that he was in serious hot water with me. I had already devised a plan for getting out of the house. I called one of my friends, Tina, to come get me. I was just waiting for him to come through the door with my baby.

When he laid Little D down for a nap, I snatched my baby up and headed for the door and yelled back, "I will see your behind in divorce court."

I stayed with Tina for a few days until I could cool off. Then I used Tina's car to drive back home so that I could at least try to talk to Danny. When I pulled up, I could not believe my eyes! My Mercedes

Benz was ashes and molten metal. Danny had set it on fire. I didn't know whether to get out of the car or keep going. Danny had lost his mind. I had no idea what to expect when I went inside the house.

With my heart racing in my chest, I walked into the kitchen. Right on the kitchen counter was the engine of my car. "Who does that? He has lost his ever-loving mind."

I figured he was at work and called his construction company. At first his secretary gave me the run around. When he finally picked up the phone, he wouldn't let me say anything. He said, "Sonja, I am not giving you a divorce."

"Are you crazy?" I said. "What in the world are you thinking? You are supposed to sleep with the 13-year-old babysitter and that is okay?"

He said, "Sonja, how do you think you are going to make it if you leave? You are not going to be able to survive. I am not going to give you any money."

"Trust me, I will make it. I made it before I met you, I will make it after you. Little D and I will be just fine.

"Sonja, if you leave, you will leave alone. You are not taking the baby with you."

When he said I couldn't take Little D with me, I just hung up the phone. My body fell against the kitchen wall and I slid down to the floor. I was crying so hard that I could barely catch my breath. I couldn't grasp what had happened over the last few weeks. My perfect world had just crumbled into pieces like an overturned jigsaw puzzle and I had no idea how to put the pieces together. Everything around me was about to change. This thirteen-year-old girl had come into my life and rocked the foundation of my world like a bulldozer, and I never saw it coming.

"Let not the oppressed return dishonored; let the afflicted and needy praise Your name" Psalm 74:21

Chapter Six

An Outside Baby, Brings Inside Pain

Finding out that Remanda was pregnant with my husband's baby was like running into a brick wall. I kept moving, but a part of me wanted to fall apart.

I had so many emotions that were running through me. I felt betrayed, deceived, and so many other things that I couldn't even begin to put them all together.

I must admit, the first time I saw Remanda after I heard about the baby was difficult. I didn't know what to say to her because she was a kid. On the other hand, I had to address her because now, she was wearing the shoes of a woman. She had come between me and the man that I had a covenant relationship with. No matter how hard this was, I knew that I was going to have to deal with her head on.

I was trying to keep peace and harmony in this horribly stressful situation. I decided to buy a few things for the baby she was carrying. I got a bassinet, some blankets and other essentials for a newborn. I packed them all up and took them to her house.

I pulled up to her house, and I felt a knot in middle of my stomach. I knew that this was going to be one of the most difficult things I would ever have to do since I had been married to Danny. I took a deep breath, and then I walked up to her front door. Her mother opened the door and met me with her cold stare. Biting my lower lip, I asked, "Can I please speak to Remanda?"

"Don't you think that yawl have done enough?" she asked with her eyebrows raised.

I didn't respond because I knew that this was a meeting that was going to have to happen. God was going to have to work this out.

I knew that her mother had to realize that I had only wanted the best for Remanda. I treated her like my little sister. I had opened the door of my home to her because I wanted her to have a better life.

Just then, her mother stepped back and called Remanda to the door. Waiting for Remanda seemed like eternity. I thought I knew what I was going to say, but now I wasn't sure.

As I was going over what our dialogue might sound like in my mind, Remanda finally appeared. We both just looked at each other for a moment. Then I broke the silence. I said, "I don't know what happened. I don't know how it happened. I just know that Danny is my husband."

Then I paused, and added, "I just want you to know that we are going to help take care of the baby." I heard her mother in the background. She said, "Un hum, whatever."

Remanda tried to explain, but none of it made sense. Finally, she took the items I had bought for the baby, thanked me, and I turned and walked back to my car.

As I left Remanda's house, I knew that a lot of people weren't happy that I decided to stay with Danny. But they didn't understand that in my parents' 26 years of marriage, I watched my mother take in outside babies all the time. I felt a man having a baby out of wedlock wasn't a reason to leave. But when the person that he was having the baby with was a child, I suppose that did make it a different story.

For a while Danny and I were trying to make the marriage work. Then one day I was trying to reach him, and he wasn't answering the phone. Back then cell phones were about a foot long, so I knew that he realized I was calling him. My female intuition made me feel that something was up. I got in the car and headed to Remanda's house in Murfreesboro. Sure enough, as soon as I pulled up in front of her house, I saw his car. I was so hot that I could have exploded.

I tried to pull myself together as I went to her front door. I rang the doorbell. When he came to the door, I asked him to come outside. Instead of responding with respect, he got cocky with me and asked, "What do you want, Sonja?"

By this time, I thought a blood vessel had burst in my brain. He had the door cracked. I pushed it open, balled up my fist and popped him in the chest. He pushed me back and tried to run to his car. I grabbed his arm and drug him down the last few steps. When he finally got away from me, he opened the door to his car. As he pulled off, I jumped on the hood of the car and made him run into the side of a building.

I think that is when people in Murfreesboro started saying that they thought I was crazy, but no one knew what was motivating my actions.

This would not be the only dramatic situation that I would encounter dealing with our "outside baby."

I had started out hanging out at a local arcade to escape some of the things that were going on in my personal life. One day I was playing one of the machines in the arcade and Remanda's stepfather walked in and started fussing. The first words out of his mouth were, "That low down dirty husband of yours he thinks he can…."

Before he finished his sentence, he pulled out a gun and started shooting at me! People started running out of the arcade and leaping into the street. One of my friends whisked me out of the back door. By the time I got to my car, he had already shot holes in it.

For a moment all I could do was stand there and look at the holes in my car. I knew they could in no way be compared to the ones that were in my heart. My heart was numb and almost void of feeling. I hadn't done anything wrong, but it seemed I was getting the brunt of this situation. An old woman had tried to hit me with her cane in the club, now I was being shot at while in the arcade. No one seemed to realize that I wasn't the one at fault, but I seemed to be an easy target. I suppose they knew what "one flesh" meant even if my husband didn't. To me my decision wasn't difficult, he was my husband, and I was going to stand by my man – even if it killed me.

Our Marriage Takes another Hit

As Remanda's due date approached it seemed that our marriage was on an emotional roller coaster. I wanted to be accepting and understanding, but the truth was I had a toddler of my own at home. I needed some acceptance and understanding myself.

Then on August 1st, Danny had decided to take me out to dinner for my birthday. He was working late so we thought it would be best just to meet at the restaurant. Deep inside, I was hoping that maybe this night would help to rekindle some of the fire that had been lost through this ordeal.

When we got to the restaurant, we ordered some appetizers. I was ready to relax and celebrate the evening with my husband. Then Danny's cell phone rang.

He picked it up. When he said that he needed to step away for a minute, I didn't think much of it. He owned his own construction company. There were many times that issues came up that he had to handle after hours. Once the waiter came by for our order, I let him know what we both wanted. To my surprise, Danny had already ordered a bottle of wine. I knew this was going to be a night to remember.

I was thinking how grateful I was that this entire situation with Remanda was almost over. Then I looked up and noticed that Danny was coming back to the table.

Before he could even sit down, he said, "Sonja, I am going to have to leave. Remanda is in labor."

His words were a little unsettling. A part of me felt a relief, but I another part of me felt a bit of anxiety. This was the moment that we had been anticipating for months. It was finally here, but something wasn't connecting.

Then, I said, "I wanna go to the hospital too."

I never in my wildest dreams thought I would hear the response that I got next.

"Sonja, they don't want you there," he picked up the check off the table.

I was devastated, I said, "What do you mean they don't want me there? I have stood by you this entire time. They want my money, but they don't want me there?"

Danny didn't even wait to hear the rest of my objection. He grabbed the check and headed toward the door. He didn't even say good-bye. He just left.

I just sat there alone trying to gather my composure. What type of birthday gift was this? The "outside baby" was being born on my birthday. Was this a sick joke? What are the chances of something like this happening? Was this designed for me to curse the day I was born? There was no way that I could figure all this out.

After a few minutes, I pulled myself together. I didn't know the answer to a lot of my questions, but I knew one thing: I was going to the hospital. The entire time I was heading to the hospital, I was hoping that I would have the strength to deal with whatever was going to happen next.

When I got to the hospital, I stopped at the nurse's station to find out which room was Remanda's room. I didn't realize since she was a minor, they would have her under an anonymous name. Now, I knew this wasn't going to be as easy as I thought it would be. Yet, I wasn't going to be outdone. I went into every room in the maternity ward. I knew at some point I would find them.

Then, I turned the corner and I saw Danny standing outside the door of a room. I knew that was her room. I heard the baby crying. While I was roving around the hospital looking for them, the baby had been born. I don't know why but I almost fainted, when I saw him somehow my worst nightmare was now a reality.

As I walked toward him, I tried to keep from falling over, because I felt my knees were going to buckle under me. Then one of the nurses came out of the room, and said to Danny, "Baby Steven is doing just fine."

Now that was the last straw! Danny and I had already decided that if we had another baby, we were going to name him Steven. I was so angry, that I thought my heart was going to jump out of my chest. This was the ultimate slap in my face. Was this the reward for being a faithful wife?

I was trying to keep my composure, but this was it. From this point, it was on and popping. I ran up to Danny and punched him in the chest. He grabbed me to try to keep me from hitting him. Before he could stop me, I hit him again.   Then he pushed me away. I fell against some shelves and they went tumbling down. I got up and started running toward him again. By this time, they had called the hospital security. I beat him until they arrived!

There is no doubt that this would be a birthday that I would never forget. This was the first time that I would go to jail. I was charged with destruction of property, assault and battery and disturbing the peace. These three charges would be the beginning of a downward spiral. I attempted to medicate a pain that was much too deep to reach.

"For great is the LORD, and greatly to be praised: he also is to be feared above all gods." 1 Chronicles 16:25 (KJV)

Chapter Seven

Drugs Began to Drag me Down

I think that my drug addiction got out of control kind of early in the game. My heart was hurting from my husband's adulterous affair. To top things off his love child was born on my birthday, and he named him the name we had selected for our next child. Losing my man to a thirteen-year-old girl, made me feel less than a woman.

There are only a few words that described the emotions I was wrestling with: loneliness, feeling unloved and low self-esteem. All these things rolled into one, left me numb. There was a void deep in my soul that nothing could fill. After a while, the dark deep pit within my inner being began to call out my name. It was like a voice from the grave wooing me into darkness.

All the people that I was clubbing with were doing drugs. I found out early on that I was allergic to marijuana, so that wasn't an option for me. I didn't drink because I had seen what alcohol had done to my mother. Instead of doing drugs, I was always the one that was bouncing around the club with a natural high. When we were hanging out all I wanted to do was dance, pop my fingers and shake my groove thang.

One night we went clubbing. I walked in the joint like I owned the place. I told the girls that I was hanging with, "I am not buying nothing unless you let me try some."

As they were passing the cigarette laced with cocaine around, they didn't have a problem giving me a hit. After all, I was financing their fun.

But to my surprise, I didn't feel anything after my first hit. I just jumped up from the table and said, "I can't believe yawl wasting my money on this mess. "I threw my money on the table. Then I headed straight to the dance floor. I didn't feel anything. I got a bigger buzz off just listening to music and dancing. I knew that cocaine had gone to their heads, and they were crazy.

Snapping my fingers in the air, I started shaking my hips toward the nearest man on the dance floor. I was shouting out "Oh yeah, let's get this party started." I knew it was time to push things to another level, and cocaine wasn't going to get me there.

Little did I realize, that was my window of escape? The Bible states, I Corinthians 10:13 "No temptation has overtaken you except such as is common to man; but God *is* faithful, who will not allow you to be tempted beyond what you are able, but with the temptation will also make the way of escape, that you may be able to bare *it.* "

Most people will probably not be able to understand what happened next. Looking from the outside in, it would be easy to say, "It takes a stupid person to do it again."

I guess my momma was right, because she would always say, "I was the dumbest, and the smartest child she had." At the time when she said it, I didn't understand what she meant. It seemed confusing. How could I be the dumbest and the smartest at the same time? Now I realized that she was saying, I was the smartest child, but I made some of the dumbest choices.

That next day, I was about to make a very dumb choice that would change my life for what seemed like eternity. I decided to try cocaine again. This time when I tried it, I liked it. I got high all day long. They kept passing the cigarette around me, and I got caught up in the smoke. The white powdered substance that was inside the cigarette was luring me in like a warm blanket on a cold night. With every puff I escaped into a land of euphoria where nothing else mattered. I didn't feel any pain. I didn't feel any anger, I didn't feel any neglect. Somehow inhaling the cocaine had hidden my hurt.

It's amazing how being around the wrong friends can get you into a destructive situation. One day of doing the wrong thing redirected the entire course of my life.

All the things that were happening to me really didn't have anything to do with me at all, but I didn't know it. I was disappointed, ashamed and I felt embarrassed. How could I have let a little girl come in and steal my man? What kind of woman was I? What was I doing when she was screwing my husband? I didn't want to deal with the hand that God had given me. Cocaine gave me a way to cop out. With a puff of a cigarette, I could opt out of life.

I started out rolling cocaine in cigarettes. They used to call them "Jimmies." I did cigarettes for years, every now and then I would do a line, but I didn't snort coke too often. I just didn't like putting it up my nose and having a running nose – that was just nasty to me.

It started out simple, but it didn't take long for my habit to catch up with me. By the time, I really started getting high my husband and his family cut me off financially. They even took my son away from me. My husband would do anything to please his parents, so he allowed his folks to take my child. Even though he didn't mind them stepping into the middle of our custody battle, he still wanted a relationship with me. But I didn't want to be with him. So, he kept stringing me along by making me have sex with him to see our son.

Before I knew it, I was caught up in this weird vicious cycle. Left helpless and out of control, I had no fight left but I had to escape. My addiction got out of control. In no time, I was getting high more and more. And my money was becoming less and less. I no longer had the limitless resources.

Battling to see my son and trying to accept the new baby that my husband, had made me feel like an outsider in my own family. There was a part of me that felt alone; I just didn't feel loved. But when I got high none of that mattered, because then I loved myself. The more things started to go wrong in my life, the more I got high. When I got high, I loved me, and it didn't matter if no one else did. I stayed high and it escalated from there.

After the "outside baby" was born, something in me died. I tried hard to act like everything was okay, but it wasn't. It was hard for me to continue to live a lie. One day I had enough, and I called one my girlfriends and asked her to come and get me and Little D.

I had reached the end of my rope. I was tired of trying to pretend like everything was okay and it wasn't. I was helping Danny support the new baby. We were buying clothes, pampers, baby food, and formula for another household. All the time, I had a baby staring me in the face. This just didn't make sense to me. It was more than I could handle. Deep inside, I realized I was only repeating what I had watched growing up. My mother was always welcoming one of my father's love children in our household. Now I was doing the same thing. I had become the victim of a generational curse.

When my girlfriend pulled up, she didn't bother coming in, she just honked the horn for me to come out. That was all the sign I needed. I grabbed Little D with one hand and my luggage with the other. Not even caring to look back, we headed toward the car. Opening the door, I hopped in. I just knew if I could get to my mama things would be better.

We pulled up to my mama's house, I swooped Little D up in my arms and we headed to the door.

When my mom saw us, she looked like she had seen a ghost. Of course, this wasn't the warm greeting that I was expecting.

"Hey girl, what yawl doing here?" she asked through a crack in the door.

I pushed the screen door open, "Mama, we need a place to stay."

I wish that I could read people better because I should've been able to realize that we weren't welcome. She didn't seem like she wanted us around, but she let us in the house anyway.

I don't even think the door shut before my mother's phone rang. She didn't tell me who it was, she just handed me the receiver. I knew then, it had to be Danny. I braced myself, for whatever he had to say, because I knew that I wasn't going back.

"What in the word are you doing?" he yelled. "You bring my baby back."

I guess he realized that wasn't going to get my attention. After he calmed down, he began to apologize, "I love you and I am not going to mess with that girl anymore." I didn't want those to be the magic words, but I knew I didn't feel welcome at my mother's house. Something had to give.

When I hung up, my mother looked at me with unsettledness in her eyes. She said, "Candy, I hate to tell you this, but I don't have room for you and the baby."

I had no choice; I had to go back to Danny. Somehow, I had to try to make things work. I didn't have any options.

Once I got back and got settled, things went from weird to ridiculous. One day two guys who looked like they worked for the FBI showed up at my doorstep. When I opened the door, he said, "I am looking for Mrs. Crutchfield."

Wondering what in the world he wanted, I said, "I am Mrs. Crutchfield."

He showed me his identification card from the bank and said, "I need your credit cards."

This was like something you would see in the movies. I guess I should have asked what for, but without questioning him I went digging in my purse. I got my credit cards out of my wallet and handed them to him. I could feel a pain in my hand and a jab in my heart as I handed my credit cards to these complete strangers. Before I could ask him, what was wrong, he took this sharp device out of his pocket that looked like scissors and proceeded to rip up my credit cards up one by one.

My mouth was hanging wide open as I watched this happen. I would later learn this was just another one of Danny's ways of controlling me. Where was I going to go without any money? They were always trying some new ploy to train me and make me line up with their perception of what a wife was supposed to be like, but they kept forgetting I wasn't the trainable type.

With fewer finances at my fingertips and my $1k-a-day habit, I began to do things to create a cash flow. I started writing hot checks, stealing from stores, and boosting things that other people stole. But I never got into prostitution. God protected me from myself when I was high. When I got high, my flesh would crawl whenever someone would touch it, so selling my body or being promiscuous was not even an option. I have a very high sex drive, but when I was high, I didn't want sex. Cocaine was my lover.

Before I knew it, I was a part of a vicious cycle. I would get high to escape my situation. Then I would abstain so that I could see my kid. I knew that my husband would want sex, and I had to stay clean if I wanted to see Little D. After I saw my son, I would get high again.

My drug addiction seemed so out of place in my family. There was nobody that I could trace in my family that had done drugs. They might have gotten drunk or smoked a little pot, but nobody did any hard-core drugs. I came from a family of Bible-based believers. They were preachers, teachers and evangelist in my family, but no addicts. Then here I come along and jumped into the pits of Hell. I became the source of many prayer meetings and altar calls for my family; everybody was trying to save me, but me.

I coasted along with cocaine for a while, and then my desire to go higher got stronger. After about two years, I "graduated" from powdered cocaine to crack. When a person smokes crack, the cocaine reaches the brain much faster. Crack gives you a higher high and a lower low. It is like somebody taking you to a mountain top, and then kicking you down to the valley. You keep trying to get back to the mountain top, and then before you know it you are back in the valley. This up and down rotation makes you crave it like a baby who craves milk. As the old saying goes, "once you do crack, you got to go back."

There were days I would get up and say, "I am *not* going to get high." That would only last for a few fleeting moments. By the end of the day I would end up with a "stem" in my mouth and I would be hitting a rock.

"Bless the LORD, O my soul: and all that is within me, bless his holy name." **Psalm 103:1** KJV

Chapter Eight

Someone Makes Me Feel Special

In the middle of my madness, I met a man who flashed a ray of hope before my eyes like a bead of sunshine.

In the years I was getting high, everyone liked to hang out at the arcade on Friday nights. I always enjoyed being around people, so I found myself gravitating to where the crowds were. Even when I was doing drugs, I never like to zone out and be by myself. I guess that made me a little unique. For the most part, I was what you would call an active junkie. I didn't like to geek out and be alone.

One night I was sitting in the arcade playing Pac Man. I had a little buzz on so the balls bouncing around making noises put me on edge a little. I also enjoyed seeing the numbers go up on the game board. Besides doing drugs, playing Pac Man was my next adrenaline rush.

I was so into the game that I didn't notice the owner was standing right by my side. I had just made some many points in the game that I had advanced to another level. I was so excited. Like a kid, my head was bopping, and I was bouncing with joy. Just when I thought I was going to win another free round, my last Pac Man died. I jumped up and hit the side of the machine, "Dang, I can't believe I lost."

The owner, whose name was Charles decided to use this opportunity to make himself known to me. Placing his hand on mine, He said, "Don't worry about it, sweetheart. I'll put some more money in the machine, so that you can keep playing. If I am here, you never have to worry about running out of money."

He slipped a few coins in the change slot. Then he rubbed his hand against mine as he continued to stand by me. His generosity had gotten my attention. My mother had always taught me to always recognize someone that showed me kindness, because folks didn't have to treat you well. As I continued to play, I said, "Thank you for letting me get my game on."

He just laughed and brushed his hand against mine one more time. By this time, I could tell his gesture was not just kindness, he was trying to flirt with me. I flashed him another big grin, hoping that it would motivate him to keep the cash coming. That night I jumped from one machine to the next. As soon as the game finished, Charles made sure another coin was added.

When I finished my last game, I stopped by the counter, "Thanks for supporting my addiction to Pac Man."

Looking at me with his bubbling brown eyes, Charles said, "You just make sure you come back." There was something about the look in his eyes and the way he made me feel, I knew I would be back soon.

After a while I became a frequent visitor of the arcade. I wouldn't just stop by in the evening; I started coming during the day. It didn't matter

"Oh, Candy, you are mistaken. Everybody loves you."

"I wish that was true, but I can give you a list as long as this room of people that couldn't care less if I were dead or alive."

My low self-esteem upset Charles. He grabbed me and squeezed me as tight as he could. He kissed my cheek "I don't ever want to hear you say those words again. I love you, and that is all that matters."

It didn't take long for him to lock the door and put out a sign saying: *Will be back soon.*

He escorted me to the back room, and he began to make love to me. This was not sex, it was love. It touched me like every moment counted, not like he was trying to take care of need. It seemed to matter to him that I had needs. I hadn't been with anyone other than my husband in years. It was wonderful to have someone touch me as more than an obligation, but a desire. I got caught up in his caresses. Every ounce of my femininity embraced his advances toward me.

When I came out of the back room of the arcade, I felt renewed. Charles was the answer to my unspoken prayers. I needed someone to show me that they loved me enough to care.

For a while it seemed that Charles was a perfect solution to my situation. He had plenty of money, and my husband had cut me off. He was not afraid to show me that he cared about me. Being around him made me feel like I was on top of the world. There was only one small problem— Charles was married.

He had fed me the same lines that all married men use: his wife didn't understand him, she didn't show him any attention, and they had grown apart. All those lines worked for me, because I needed someone to show me some love.

One night, I stopped by the arcade right before he was about to close. I was wearing a pretty pink top and some designer blue jeans. Charles reached behind the counter and took out his camera. He began to snap pictures of me like I was a super model like Tyra Banks. I love the attention that he was giving me. I started posing and smiling.

I jumped up on one of the arcade machines, tossed my head back and said, "How you like me now?"

He just laughed and kept snapping away. "Turn your head to the left, give me a smile, drop your chin a little," he instructed.

We both lost track of time. By the time he finished snapping his camera, he started to focus on me. He put his camera behind the counter again.

The next thing I knew it was morning.

A few days later I came in the arcade, and there was a huge 16x20 picture of me plastered on the wall behind the counter. It was positioned right behind the cash register so that everyone could see it. When I saw that picture, I knew he had lost his mind.

I took one look at the picture, and I came unglued. "Man, what in the world is your wife going to do when she sees this picture?"

I couldn't believe that he had the nerve to place a picture of me in his place of business.

"I don't care what she says, you are beautiful, and I want the world to know it."

"You are crazy. She is going to kill you."

We both laughed. I didn't think much more of it until I came in and saw the picture was no longer hanging on the wall. I canvassed the room with my eyes to see where it had been moved. I noticed it was lying ripped into several pieces behind the counter.

I smiled when I saw it. Walking over to Charles, I said, "I guess Missy found out you been messing around."

Patting me on the butt, he said, "And that am not going to stop nothing. She will just have to deal with it."

It didn't take me long to realize that Charles was a man of his word. Before long he had another picture of me hanging up, like there wasn't a problem. After a while his love for me made me cocky. He would do whatever I said, and he would give me whatever I asked for.

Sometimes I would fight him to get what I wanted. One time I got mad, because he wouldn't give me any cash, so I bit him in the stomach. I bit down on him with my mouth that my tooth prints were left in the side of his stomach.

One night I was hard up. I needed some cash to get some more crack. I marched into the arcade like I owned the place.

"Give me some money, man. "

Charles didn't want me to do drugs, so he ignored my request.

I needed to get high. "Charles, I am not playing with you. Man, give me some money."

"Girl, you need to leave that stuff alone. You are better than that."

I knew that I didn't need his lectures, I needed drugs.

I reached behind the counter and pushed the cash register on the ground. The cash drawer flew open when the register hit the ground. I reached in the cash draw and got some money and headed out the door.

As I was running down the street, I heard him yelling after me, "Don't let those drugs drag you down. Girl you got too much going for you."

When I was getting high, I kept hearing Charles' voice echoing in my head, "Girl you got too much going for you. "

As I zoned out, with my last hit on the pipe, I could not block out his words of encouragement: *You need to go back to school, you are special, you are better than this.*

Deep in my soul, I knew Charles was right. I just didn't know how to make his words my reality. Charles was trying to tell me I was special, and the devil was trying to destroy me. I couldn't hear his message, because I was still drowning in my misery.

"I thank and praise you, God of my ancestors: You have given me wisdom and power, you have made known to me what we asked of you, you have made known to us the dream of the king." Daniel 2:23

Chapter Nine

My Love Child Brings Me Joy

When I found out that I was pregnant, it only complicated my situation. I was still doing crack, I was still trying to see my son when I could, and I was still sleeping with my husband, Danny.

I had something growing inside me and my self-esteem had hit a new low.

Before I even took a pregnancy test, Charles confronted me. One day I was in the arcade playing one of the machines like I always did. He came up behind me and placed his hands on my stomach. "Girl, I think you are carrying a little something extra with you."

I just brushed his hands away. "You wish, "I said, not taking my attention away from the game machine.

He placed his hands-on top of mine. This time I knew that he was not playing. "I am serious, Candy, you need to take a pregnancy test. I think you're pregnant. If you are, you're going to have to leave that stuff alone."

He stepped back and added, "I felt it when it happened. Candy, you can't get high anymore."

I stopped playing my game and turned my head toward him. His eyes were piercing as he looked at me. There was no doubt in my mind that he meant what he was saying, but I knew he couldn't be right. I jumped back from the machine. "I'll take the test if you want, but there is no way that you felt that."

The next day, I wanted to get high so bad, but I went to the county doctor instead. Charles' accusations were correct. Sure, enough I was pregnant. I was only two months when I found out. I went cold turkey from drugs.

The next 7 months, I did not touch any drugs. It was the longest seven months of my life. Every chance he got, Charles was getting me food, buying me milk, and making me take vitamins.

When I would stop in the arcade, he would say, "Candy, you got to take care of yourself. There's more than just you that you need to be concerned about now."

He felt like me being pregnant was a chance for me to make a change in my life. "You can go back to school, when the baby is born, and get your life back on track," he encouraged.

I didn't want to change, so I just let what he was saying go in on ear and out the other. I wanted to get back to doing crack so bad that I could taste it. Unlike most crack addicts, I wasn't willing to do drugs at any cost. I knew that for me to have a healthy baby, I had to leave the drugs alone. I set my crack pipe aside.

I was full of emotion. I hadn't been drug-free this long in years, but I had a lot of things going on in my head. I was still sleeping with my husband Danny, and I was going with a married man, Charles.

When it was time for me to give birth, it was crazy because I didn't know whose baby it was. I called my mom to the hospital. We didn't know if it was Danny's baby or Charles' love child. Both were saying it was theirs. It was embarrassing.

Since I was sleeping with both, it could be either one. They both showed up to the hospital. Since I was still married, the baby was going to have Danny's last name, Crutchfield.

I was so confused that I had my mother go into the delivery room with me – she knew about both men. I had a Cesarean section. When they first pulled the baby out, my mother yelled, "Oh my God, that's Charles' baby!" She paused with a puzzled expression, "No, it's probably Danny's." Then she threw her hands up, "Candy, I am sorry, I don't know whose baby this is."

I saw the way the nurse looked at me, as my mother began to motion between Danny and Charles as the potential father of my new baby girl. It was embarrassing, but true; I had two men in the waiting room and they both were willing to claim my nine-pound, bouncing baby girl. She looked like Charles, but both men were claiming her.

My daddy drama was more than I could take. I should have been excited to be a new mother, but all I wanted to do was get high. I had told Charles to roll me a Jimmie and bring it to the hospital. He loved me so much he'd do anything I asked.

When he walked in the room, I didn't say anything about the baby. "Hey, where is my stuff."

He reached in his pocket and pulled out a cigarette pack with my cocaine laced cigarette.

Charles helped me put my robe on. I slipped my feet in my slippers and headed down the hall while Charles stayed in the room. I had to find a place to get high. The hospital was aware of my previous drug use. They had tested me when I had been admitted and I had been clean. My baby was born without any drugs in her system. Now, I was ready to take my first hit in 7 months.

My body was twitching as I walked down the hallway looking for a place to get high. There wasn't any place on my floor. I opened the door to the stairwell and went down one flight of stairs. My body was still weak from the delivery, but I needed a hit so bad.

I kept walking and looking for just the right spot. Then I saw a member of maintenance come out of a door with a sponge and bucket in his hands. As soon, as he was out of sight, I opened the door. The maintenance closet would be the perfect place for me to smoke my crack. I locked the door from the inside so no one would walk in on me. I sat on the floor next to the sponges and dirty rags. My hand was shaking as I pulled out the plastic bag with the Jimmie and my cigarette lighter.

My fingers were shaking as I brought the lit cigarette to my lips. I took one puff and it was ecstasy. I puffed my way into a state of euphoria. The odor from the cigarette was strong. I was hoping I could get back to my room before anyone discovered that I was missing.

When I finished, I pulled myself together and staggered down the hallway back to my room on the next floor.

When I got in bed, I acted like nothing was wrong. But the staff knew something was up. When the nurse came in to take my vital signs, she was in shock.

She looked at the machine and then she looked at me. She looked at the machine again. "Mrs. Crutchfield, this can't be right. I'm going to have to take your vital signs again."

She took them again and shook her head. "We are not going to be able to bring the baby in until we can get your vital signs under control."

I was too high to really care. "Okay, whatever you say, Miss Nurse." I turned over and enjoyed the feeling that I had been missing for several months.

Giving birth only added to chaotic situation that I was in. I had two men that were eager about being the father of my daughter. I didn't even have custody of my son. Now my mother was going to have to step in and keep my daughter. I was returning to my first love – crack.

A Rough Encounter

A few years after my daughter was born, I met Charles' wife. By this time my daughter was about three-years-old and we knew she belonged to Charles. We were in the grocery store. My daughter spotted Charles and started pulling on my arm, "There is my daddy."

I began to walk toward him, but he had this scared look on his face. I looked past him and noticed his wife was with him. I tried to pull Sontoya back, but she wasn't having it.

She yanked my arm in the direction of Charles. "I want my daddy," she announced.

His wife looked at me with pure rage in her eyes. Charles and I were still seeing each other at the time but he had told her that the child wasn't his. I knew that when she took one look at my daughter, she knew it was Charles' baby. He was seeing us as much as he could outside of his marriage.

His wife turned toward him. "Pay her whatever she wants. That baby has you all over her." She turned and walked away.

If I had met her first, I would have never messed with him. She was the sweetest woman I had ever met. She wrote out the child support checks and gave me some of the prettiest gifts for my daughter. She made sure that Sontoya didn't have to want for anything. With the clothes she provided, my daughter always looked like a princess.

One day I got a chance to sit down and talk to her. "You can hate me all you want, but I am not going to hate you. I refuse to do that. I am not going to heaven and can't get in because of something that I am holding against somebody," I told her with great conviction in my spirit.

My feelings toward her were genuine. I knew she felt betrayed, but she tolerated me so that she could help with my daughter.

I wished that I could say having my daughter made me get on track, but it didn't. My mother ended up keeping my baby, because I couldn't stop getting high.

Standing at the Door of Heaven

A guy offered to fund my high. He had gotten some back pay from social security and liked having me around. He had more drugs than I had seen anyone with, unless they were dealing it. In a fit of drug-induced paranoia, he got so high that he put the refrigerator in front of the door. He thought that someone was going to come in on us try to steal our drugs.

He had so much dope that he wanted to smoke it as fast as possible. I wasn't used to smoking fast and when I tried to take my time, it made him more paranoid. "Are you the police, why you aren't' hitting it?" he asked.

I couldn't believe that he was tripping this hard. "Man, I have known you for years. You know I am not a fast smoker. All this money you spend on dope, you ought to let me enjoy it," I said.

He kept going, "Shhhhhhhh, be quiet. Did you hear that?"

If it wasn't for the fact that he had bought the drugs, I would have said, *No, I didn't hear that! You crazy.* Since, he had all the money and all the dope; I kept smoking as fast as I could.

I was smoking so fast that I could literally see my heart pounding in my chest.

In those days if someone overdosed, they'd be dragged outside. Nobody wanted to get caught with a murder charge, and of course you didn't want the police snooping around. When I passed out from taking in too much crack, he pulled my lifeless body outside onto the sidewalk.

I died that night. In my mind, I had a vivid picture of what happened next. I got to heaven and couldn't get in. When I went up, all I could see was this bright, beautiful gate.

I could hear the voice of God speaking in the background. His voice sounded like rolling waters. Jesus was standing at the gate in my defense, but God said, "She can't come in here."

I couldn't believe it. I was right at the gateway of heaven, and I wasn't going to make it in. Then I began to plead my own case. "God, I was really nice. When I was on drugs, I made sure whoever's house I got high at had food to eat. If they had kids, I gave them food and I made sure their lights were on. I have always been a giver." I pleaded.

Then Jesus jumped in and said, "Lord, she has done this, and she done that." He continued with a long list of things that even I had forgotten about.

Our attempts were not fazing God, He still said, "She can't come in here. "

I tried to tell Him again a third time. Then I could hear the cock crowing.

I really feel like if I had kept on pleading, I would be in hell today. When I heard the cock crow that third time, I said, "Okay, Okay, I don't want to come in, just let me live and I 'll get it right."

When I woke up, I was in the hospital, and I was told I had overdosed.

Somebody found me in the street and called the ambulance. Then they brought me to the hospital.

When I raised up that hospital bed ringing wet, I was sweating out of fear. That is when I realized it was time to quit.

All I could think is, *do you want to meet your Maker doing what you are doing?* No, no, I didn't want to meet my Maker getting high, or doing any kind of drugs.

My friends were praying for me, my brother was praying for me and my grandmother was praying for me. The Bible says that the "prayers of the righteous availeth much." I know they were all petitioning heaven for God to move in my life. On one hand I had prayer and the other hand I had Charles saying how special I was. Surely, special people didn't do dope. All I could do was pray that God would intervene so that I could stop this mad cycle of addiction.

.

"This poor man cried, and the LORD heard him, and saved him out of all his troubles." Psalm 34:6

Chapter Ten

Deliverance from a Dumpster

It would have been wonderful if overdosing was enough for me to turn my life around. It was a spark to help lead me in the right direction, but it was not enough to make me get my life in order. I got out of the hospital and went right back to doing drugs.

Everybody in my family knew that if I was going to survive, I had to get off crack. My grandmother would even come looking for me in the hood. Sometimes I would be standing on the corner, and I would get a tap on my shoulder. "Baby you need some money. They say that stuff cost a lot of money," she would say in her raspy voice.

The one thing that I will never forget was no matter who turned their back on me, my grandmother always told me, "Baby no matter what, you come by here I will feed you." She might not have been happy with the choices that I made, but she wasn't trying to throw me out with the dishwater.

One day I had been crashing at my grandmother's house. She said, "What's that stuff look like any way? I am going to buy you some crack." I couldn't believe my ears. I needed a fix bad. As weird as it might seem to be getting it from my grandmother, I wasn't going to pass her up on the offer.

We got in her car, and she drove me over to the hood to buy me a gram. A gram costs 40 dollars and depending on drug dealer it could be about the size of a dime. I came back to the house, ready to take a hit. The crack we purchased was rolled up in a dollar bill.

My grandmother was very inquisitive about our purchase. She unrolled the dollar bill to reveal the small rocks of crystal inside. She took her fingers and began to flick at the rock, "I can't believe that you paid $40 dollars for that little bitty mess?" I almost fainted as I saw my crystal rock fall on the floor.

To my surprise none if this fazed my grandmother, she just kept on with her questions, "Now what are you going to do with it?" she asked. When I lit up my pipe, she seemed baffled. With a puzzled look on her face she said, "It's got smoke going up in that thing. You see that?" There was no doubt that my grandmother had ruined my high. I finally gave up taking a hit and went to sleep.

I think that I could take everyone else's disappointment, but It was hard to see my grandmother's disappointment. Looking at me balled up in a corner on the couch, she said, "Baby you going to let that stuff run you like that?" She continued, "You stay gone. You don't eat, and it looks like you haven't been to sleep in a week."

When you have a drug addiction like I had, it was hard work. I had a $1,000/day habit. It is very hard to keep up with that kind of habit. You can't get it just lying on your back.

In order to support my habit, I became very business savvy. If I was boosting some jeans that I stole, I made sure I got close to what their value was. If the jeans cost $30 dollars, you had to give me at least $15 – that was not up for negotiation.

In the middle of my mess, I still didn't forget about Jesus. I would go around singing church songs. My favorite songs were: "His Eye is on the Sparrow," "I'm Still Holding On," and "Because He Lives."

The local junkies thought I was crazy, because I would be getting high singing church songs and reciting Scriptures.

I wouldn't wish a drug habit on my worst enemy. When you get to putting into dollars and cents, if I had half the money I was spending when I was on drugs, I would be a multi-millionaire. I truly believe that. Based on my $1,000-a-day-habit, I was easily blowing over $364,000 dollars a year.

In order to keep things going, I had my own little business going. If I knew today was Saturday, the banks would close Sunday. I realized that I would have to make enough money to last me until Monday.

I would supply the bootleg house with liquor, cups, and all kinds of miscellaneous stuff. I always kept a little red note pad with me. I would run through the bootleg house taking orders. Swinging my pad in pencil, I would yell out, "How much liquor all need, and how many cups you want?"

I acted like I was their supply man. I was quick to let them know how much they were going to owe me based on their purchase. What I didn't earn from boosting, I got from writing hot checks. I would case the local stores so that I knew what to take and when to take it.

I was dating a guy T.J. – he was a burglar by trade. He could go in and steal one check out of their check book. People would never close the account, because they didn't realize that the check was missing until it was too late. We would then print other checks to that account. I would memorize the person's information and it was on.

I was always in full character for whoever I was supposed to be. We had checks for this one lady that worked at the VA Hospital, so I would go into one of the local grocery stores wearing nurse's scrubs. I would get cartons of cigarettes and cases of beer. I would buy film and batteries, whatever would be easy to unload. I filled my cart to the brim. I had a lot of items that would be easy to sell.

The manager of the store took one look at me, and he knew something wasn't right. I didn't have an ID, so that asked him to verify the check. He looked me right in the eyes. "What's your name?"

I didn't blink an eye and I responded with the person's name that was on the check.

I knew that he had figured I was up to something, I put my hand on my hip and said," What's your problem, is it because I'm black." I could tell he was going to try to win this argument.

He said, "why you need all this, stuff."

I couldn't let him blow my cover. "Look, I work third shift and I just got off. I am tired." Then I really began to clown. I added, "We are having a cookout at the hospital, if it's any of your business."

I don't think he knew exactly what was wrong, but he knew something didn't jive. He just looked at me and said, "Get out of my store. "

Even though I was wrong as two left shoes, I wasn't leaving without a fight. I turned to one of the cashiers and said, "Don't I come in here all the time, sweetie?"

She smiled, "Yes ma'am."

I was counting on the fact that she saw me all the time; she just didn't realize I was someone different every time I came in. I would always go to different registers, so no one would know I was using a different person's checking account each time I came in the store.

The bottom line was that I knew the store manager had me, but I wasn't going to give in that easy. I tossed a package of cigarettes that were in my hand on the counter, I said, "You have got to be kidding me," and I headed for the door. I went straight outside to the pay phone. By this time, I was in full actor mode.

I picked up the phone and called the national headquarters for the store. I explained to the person on the other end that I felt that I was being discriminated against because I was black.

The gentleman on the phone asked if I had my identification with me. "No sir, I don't have any ID on me right now," I explained. "But I come in this store all the time. I just got off work and I have been working all night. I didn't' realize that I didn't have my ID in my purse until I got to the checkout counter."

The girl that was driving me was getting ready to leave. I put the phone down and said, "Girl, don't you leave me. I'm about to get the stuff! It's going to work. If the store manager is wrong, and I'm who I say I am, they will have a major lawsuit on their hands."

When I hung up the corporate office told me to go back into the store. I couldn't wait to go back in, and yell, "Your supervisor is about to call you."

Sure, enough the phone rang as soon as the words rolled off my lips. When the store manager picked up the phone, all I could hear was him saying, "Yes sir, yes sir, yes sir."

The cashier was still holding my two buggies full of meat, cigarettes, batteries, and cups. Before she rung me out, I turned and saw a card table in the corner of the store. Turning toward the card table I said, "As matter of fact, I just saw a table and 4 chairs over there. I want you to add that to my order as well." She sent someone to get it, and I wrote the check for the entire thing.

Once I got everything bagged up, I headed out the door. As I was putting things in the car, the girl that was waiting on me said, "Girl you are crazy, I can't believe you got away with that." I had a habit and I had to be creative to support it. This was just one time that I got over on the system, but my luck was about to run out.

One night after that incident, I was looking for a place to go to sleep. I couldn't find anybody that would let me stay with them. My own mother wouldn't let me sleep at the house. After going from place to place, I was exhausted. I found myself in an alley behind a hotel. There was a Dipsy Dumpster behind the hotel. I opened the lid and crawled inside. I didn't even have a match, so I couldn't even get high. This was probably a good thing because I would have set myself on fire with all the paper that was around me.

I snuggled up under some bags of garbage and went to sleep. When I woke up, I heard the truck picking up the dumpster. I was in shock and I began banging on the dumpster from the inside, "Hey, I am in here." I knew when they picked it up, they would toss it into the machined and I would be crushed flat as a pancake.

I was desperate to try to stop this guy; I kept banging on the dumpster as hard as I could. I kept shouting, "I'm in here, I'm in here, but my voice was not carrying."

I backed up and ran into the side of the dumpster with all my might. Then I screamed to the top of my lungs, "I'm in here, please let me out."

This time the guy heard me. The noise stopped. Then the dumpster made a loud thump as it hit the ground. The next thing I knew the lid to the dumpster lifted. "Hey, are you okay in there?" called the man who was driving the truck.

When I saw the look on his face, I could tell that he thought he had hurt me.

He extended his hand to help me get out. "What are you doing in there?"

"I didn't have anywhere to lay my head," I explained, as I lifted my body out of the dumpster.

When I got to the ground, I dusted myself off. The guy just looked at me in amazement, "Are you sure you're okay?" He asked one last time.

"Yes sir, I'll be fine. I'm just glad you didn't kill me," I called back as I walked down the alley way.

Once again God had reached in and snatched me out of a dangerous situation. He used to help me all the time. Even when I was flying high as I kite, he would give me a sign that it was time to go.

I could not believe that I was drowning in drugs and God was taking the time to try to deliver me. This time He even dove into a Dipsy Dumpster to keep me from a deadly situation. As I walked down the alley, I was feeling blessed to be alive. Little did I realize things were about to change.

"The LORD your God is with you, the Mighty Warrior who saves. He will take great delight in you; in his love he will no longer rebuke you,

but will rejoice over you with singing." Zephaniah 3:17 (NIV)

Chapter Eleven

The Saving Grace of the Jail Bars

My drug addiction was so drastic in my life that I just couldn't see myself clear. I was going from one high to the next, searching for something that I would never find. I kept trying to recapture my first high and all the time I was falling deeper and deeper into an endless pit of self-destruction. I had given everything to find that sweet sensation of my first hit and in the process had lost grasp of who I was.

After almost 14 years of coasting with crack, my entire world was crumbling around my feet. I had two children and didn't have custody of either one of them. My own mother would no longer return my phone calls. I was even banned from almost every major store in the community because of my stealing to support my habit.

I had gotten tired of living like I was living and looking like I was looking. I was so frail that my brother said I looked like death eating crackers.

I would look at myself in the mirror, and I didn't even recognize who I had become. My complexion had darkened, my cheeks were sunken in. The circle under my eyes was so dark from my many sleepless nights that it looked like they had been drawn with a black Crayola.

I just knew that I needed a change. One day, I was stumbling around the street trying my best not to get high.

I saw one of the police officers that I knew standing on the street corner. I was so bold! Even though I had just dropped some dope in my pocket, I walked up to him and asked, "Hey man, you got any BOLO (Be on the lookout for) on me?" As I was standing there I started fidgeting with the crack in my pocket. I knew that I needed to go to jail. If I stayed in the street I was going to surely die. I was so weak I don't think my body could have sustained my next hit.

The police officer was very familiar with me. He said, "Candy, we're not looking for you," and he kept looking straight ahead like I wasn't even there.

I was desperate. I had to go to jail. I took the drugs out of my pocket and waved it in front of his face. I said, "Look I got some crack. You need to arrest me for possession of an illegal substance."

He just knocked it out of my hands, stepped on it and said, "Candy, you need to go somewhere and get some rest. I don't have time to be bothered with you today."

When my drugs hit the ground, something in me snapped. I fell to the sidewalk and tried to salvage them. With tears rolling down my face, I said "Man, you crazy. You know how hard it is to get this stuff."

I paused and looked up at him. "If I had known you were going to do that, I would have smoked it."

Continuing to cry I said, "I am going to kill myself if I stay out here." I was so angry that he wouldn't take me seriously and arrest me. I just went up to his car. I pulled my foot back and kicked the door with every ounce of strength that I had left. I almost fell over as my foot went into the side of the police car. I staggered back and noticed that my foot had left a dent in the back-side door of the car.

Walking toward me, the officer took out his handcuffs. He said, "Candy, this is your lucky day. You are about to get your wish. You are going to jail."

His words were like music to my ears. I knew the drill. I put my hands behind my back. Over the last few years this had become routine for me. I had been arrested 31 times before. Going to jail was like going home for me. Opening the back door to the squad car, the police officer said, "I don't know about you girl. I tried so hard to keep from taking you to jail, but just wouldn't let me."

When he closed the door, I looked out of the window into the streets. There was a peace that ran through my body. I couldn't stay out on the streets, and now I was safe. Jail would be my solace and my one avenue for staying out of harm's way.

As we pulled up to the jailhouse, I felt something that I had never felt before. It was a strange sense of tranquility. My soul just settled down, as I entered the building, everything in me relaxed. All the time I was on crack, I was fidgeting, on edge and out of control. But walking through the corridors of the jailhouse just brought me to an inner peace. My body was exhausted. It had been almost two weeks since I had gotten any sleep. The very pores of my skin ached with pain from restlessness. I couldn't even remember the last time I had eaten a hot meal or better yet taken a shower. As crazy as it sounded, I knew that jail was exactly where I needed to be.

Without even looking up at me, the booking agent said, "Welcome home, Candy."

I just sort of smiled at her, because she realized it too. This was my home. My family prayed for me, but they didn't want any part of me. All my friends were in jail. This is where I needed to be, at least for now.

Once I went through booking, I finally got to my cell. Walking down the hallway to my cell was like a family reunion. People were yelling: *Hey Candy. What's up girl? Welcome back.*

In my cell, I was again greeted by someone I knew. It was a girl that had been locked up several times before for prostitution. I couldn't remember her name, but I will never forget her face. When she saw me, she just lit into me like a pit bull, "Hey girl, don't tell me you in here again. With your Scripture-reciting, Bible-toting self. You back in here just like the rest of us."

"Listen, I really don't want to hear nothing you got to say," I said. I fell on the hard bed in the corner of the cell, knowing I needed some rest.

Putting her hands on her hip, she continued with her smart remarks, "Oh you don't have to listen to me, girl. I want to hear from you. I just want to know what the Lord done told you now. Evidently, He didn't tell you don't smoke crack, because you are right back." Then she busted out laughing.

"Don't smoke crack, cause you right back...that sort of rhymes doesn't it?" she laughed again.

"Why don't you sing me one of those good old church songs, I am not been to church in years. Candy, you might be my blessing in disguise. I guess I need to thank God you can't stop getting high," she said still laughing.

By this time people in the cells around us were laughing as well. I could hear one of the girls in the cell next to us yell out, "Crack-smoking Candy done slipped up again. Please don't condemn us poor sinners, we know we going to hell. But girl, you the one toting the get-out-of-hell free card."

I buried my head in my pillow and tried to drown out their words. But I knew they were right. I was a walking sound board for Christ, but that didn't keep me from hitting the crack pipe. I couldn't continue to be a living and walking contradiction.

Since I couldn't get any rest, I rolled out of the bed and went to the front of the cell. I knew that Jesus knew my heart. I was determined to get it right this time. I leaned on the bars of the cell with both hands, and all the strength I could muster, I held on to the steel bars. It was almost like if I let them go, I was going to fall. I thought about how bad I wanted to be arrested. I thought about the night I overdosed and was left on the street for dead. I thought about the time I fell asleep in the Dipsy dumpster and almost got demolished. I thought about the night that God sent an angel to tell me, He had something for me to do. There was no doubt that God had more in store for me than this. He was watching out for me when I couldn't watch out for myself. My only question was where was He *now*? I needed Him to break this vicious cycle. I couldn't stop the laughter, because everything they were saying was true.

Yet, I knew amid my mess God had kept me. I could still hear people laughing in the cells near me. They were spreading the word that I was back. In my soul I cried out to God, the madness needs to stop here. This couldn't be like any of the other times that I came to jail.

Holding on to the cell bars, I listened to all the comments that the girls were making. Tears began roll down my face and dissolve into the cement floor. I kicked my shoes off. I needed a hit bad, but this one had to come straight from heaven.

I began to wiggle my toes and twitch my fingers as I was holding on to the cell bars. Then I felt this surge go through my body that felt like nothing I had ever experienced before. Suddenly, I broke out singing,

Listening to all the comments that my surrounding cell mates were making, I threw my head back and began to belt out:

Why should I feel discouraged, why should the shadows come, why should my heart be lonely, and long for heaven and home?

I could feel this stillness come over the cell as I sang. The girls stopped laughing. I could hear a few of them shouting, "Amen. Sang girl, sang!"

But, none of that mattered. I was trying to reach Jesus. My body started shaking when I finally got my heavenly connection. I just jumped up and down, as I finished the last few verses:

His eye is on the sparrow, and I know He watches me.

When I finished singing, all the girls in the cells around me were pressing their faces against the cell bars. One guard was standing in the corridors crying. I had gotten their attention, and now God was about to get mine.

"But as for me, I will declare it forever; I will sing praises to the God of Jacob." Psalm 75:9

Chapter Twelve

Turning from Crack to Christ

Although being back in jail was like coming home, there was something different about this time. I had already done the math on my sentence. I was given 2 years at 30 percent. I knew this translated into 6 months and 13 days. I figured this would give me just enough time to get myself together, so that I could get back on the street.

My first few days were the hardest for me. I had been on a 14-day drug spree before I got arrested. My body was so tired that when I went to sleep, I couldn't wake up. One of the girls in my cell joked that they had put a mirror under my noise to make sure I was still alive. Finally, one of the guards shook me to get me up. She dragged me to the shower. The drugs had started seeping out of my pores and my body was giving off a horrendous odor. When I came to myself, I was embarrassed by the stench.

As she was dragging me to the shower, one of the guards said, "Crutchfield you stink. We are going to have to put some soap and water on you and pray that will be enough."

Once I got in the shower, I let out a sigh of relief. The water tingling against my skin was just another sign that I was still alive. My body melted under the pressure of the warm water. I had not taken a bath in a while, and this felt so good.

When I got back to my cell, I felt refreshed. It didn't take me long to fall back into the routine of things. After a few weeks, I had forgotten all about the prayer that I had prayed on the side of the road a few nights before I was arrested.

I had gotten used to the jail routine. I wasn't in the middle of a crisis, so I didn't feel that I needed to be rescued from crack. My only focus now was when I was going to get out of there. Then one day when I was sitting in my cell thinking about getting out, one of the new guards came to get me.

As she unlocked the door to my cell, she said, "Inmate Crutchfield, you have a visitor." She opened the door and led me to the visitor's gallery. All the time I was walking I was wondering, *who was coming to see me?* My family had decided to give me tough love, so I knew that none of them would be coming to see me. I had burned bridges with just about everyone that I knew. No matter how hard I tried, I could not figure out who my mystery visitor might be.

Once I sat down at the booth, my mystery was solved. There was a man sitting on the other side of the booth with his hands crossed. He was a middle age man with a receding hairline. His skin was dark brown and his eyes warm and inviting. I didn't recognize him, but he was a visitor and I wasn't about to look a gift horse in the mouth. I was just happy to see somebody. I sat down and reached to pick up the receiver.

Without explaining who he was, he said, "God has something for you to do at the Tennessee prison for women."

His words sounded foreign to me, since I had never been to prison, and I didn't have any intention on going there. This entire situation was a bit baffling because I was still trying to figure out who he was. Yet, something wouldn't allow me to ask him.

Caught off guard by his statement, I replied, "Okay I am going to go there once I get out of here. I'll be out of here in a few weeks, and I will be happy to see what I can do at the prison."

He looked at me like he had not heard a word I said. Then He repeated, "God has something for you to do at the Tennessee State prison and you are going to have to go."

I didn't want to argue with him, so I nodded my head. He looked at me straight in my eyes and said, "Do you mind if I pray with you?"

In the position that I was in, I wasn't about to turn down some prayer. With a quickness, I said, "Go right ahead."

Although in many ways my life was way off track, I still had a genuine reverence for the Lord. If God said it, I knew that it was a done deal.

Over the years I had heard a lot of people pray. I had been in church since I was a little girl. I knew the power of prayer. Yet, there was unique about this prayer. Once he opened his mouth, I felt the presence of God enter the room.

When he finished praying, I opened my eyes and looked around the room. Everything within my sight looked the same, but I knew something had changed. I pulled my chair back and stood up. I thanked him for his visit, and he left.

I was standing there, a little stunned by what had just happened. Then one of the guards, named Shelly, yelled out at me, "Hey Crutchfield, what are you doing up here in the visitor's area?"

"I had a visitor," I said, pulling myself together.

I was well known for trying to get away with stuff and I knew that she didn't trust me. She looked on the roster, and said, "No, you don't have a visitor. There is no one listed down here to see you."

It was obvious that she didn't believe me, but she also knew that I couldn't have gotten to this area by myself.

A part of me wanted to convince her that I was telling the truth, because I needed to believe what had happened myself.

"Yeah, somebody just told me that I was going to prison," I responded, trying to assure her that I had been with a visitor.

Still holding the roster, she keyed in my information to the computer. With a little bit of disgust in her voice, she said, "Sonja you get out of jail in 12 days. You are *not* going to prison."

Realizing that this entire situation was a little strange, she asked, "How did you get up here?"

I responded, "The new lady brought me up here."

"We don't have a new lady," She was clearly getting annoyed.

Although I knew that she didn't believe me, I also knew that she was aware that I didn't get out here by myself. I didn't know the jail staff. All I knew was that this strange man had told me that I was going to prison.

Officer Shelly said, "Crutchfield, I don't know how you got out here, but I am going to take you back to your cell right now."

I didn't put up a fight, because this was weird to me too.

Once I got back to the unit, I couldn't wait to tell the other girls about my weird visitor. As a couple of the girls were leaning toward me, I said, "You will never believe what happened."

The girls knew I always had a dramatic story to tell. One of the girls said with a touch of sarcasm in her voice, "No, what?"

I didn't pay her any attention, because I knew that this story was going to have them rocking. With my somewhat captive audience, I began to recall the recent events. "This guy came to visit me, and he said that I am going to TPW, because God has something for me to do."

One of the girls in the cell next to me yelled out, "Candy you need to cut all the crap out. You know you not supposed to go to prison. In fact, you are getting out of here before I am."

I knew that she was making fun of me, but I had to figure out what was going on. I had never been to prison, and the idea of going was downright frightening. I had done a lot of crimes, but they were little crimes; the people that were in prison had done major crimes. I knew that the ladies that were behind penitentiary bars were career criminals.

After I had shared my story, I got quiet in a corner of my cell. I began to cry. I had been in jail over 30 times, and it was a piece of cake. I had never been to prison. But I had heard some of the stories that other ladies had shared. I knew that prison was not for me. With tears running down my face, I cried out to God, "I don't want to go to prison. I am scared."

The next day they called a list of girls that were going to prison. My name wasn't on that list. Now, I was the laughingstock of the jail. Yolanda, who had been to jail about as many times as I had begun to make fun of me.

"Candy, every time you come to jail you teach the Bible to us. You preach to us like we were in Sunday school. You tell us that we need to do this, and we need to do that. Then you get out and you smoke as much dope as the rest of us," she spouted off.

She paused and added; "Now you say that God is sending you to prison, and you aren't even going. What kind of God is that?"

I listened to her because I knew that some of what she was saying was right. Yet, I knew this guy had said that I was going to prison. I really believed that it was a divine meeting.

The other girls began to listen and started to chime in with Yolanda. I tolerated their comments, but it was torture inside. I knew that God had visited me, and it was now up to Him to resolve this mystery.

Once the chatter quieted, I turned my head to the cell wall. With a deep conviction in my soul, I said, "Lord there are non-believers. If you still want me to go to prison send me. "

The next day bright and early, I heard the cell bars rattling. One of the guards was coming to get me. With a slight chuckle in her voice, she said, "Crutchfield, I guess you're going to get your wish after all. You're going to prison."

Walking down the corridor with her, I couldn't believe it. Everyone had assured me that I was misunderstood. I wasn't going to prison. The other girls headed to prison boarded the bus yesterday. I knew there wasn't another bus scheduled to go to the Prison for months.

All the time I was walking down the hall, I felt like screaming, "God, can't you take a joke. I'm not ready to go prison. I was sort of dragging my feet as they moved me down the hall. When the door opened, I saw a white unmarked police car waiting for me like a chariot to take me to my next destination. They placed me in the back seat of the car, and I was off to my new home, the Tennessee State Prison for Women in Nashville, TN.

My mind was racing the entire time during the 45-minute drive. This was a big mistake, but I didn't know how to stop it. A perfect stranger had already prophesied it to me just a few days prior to this chain of events.

The only thing that made this situation worse was when I finally got to the state prison, they did not have my name on their logs for the day. I had to sit in intake all day long. They didn't want to admit me because I wasn't on their roster. They called back to Rutherford County jail, and the county jail didn't want to take me back. I guess they figured they had gotten rid of me, now I was the prison's problem.

I could hear them going back and forth, but no one seemed to have the answer to the question: *where I should be?*

Then there was a shift change. I was tired and frustrated when I saw this new woman take over the front desk. I walked over to her because I knew that I didn't have anything to lose. Feeling like I was at the end of my rope, I said, "I don't know if you believe in God or not, but there was a man that came to see me the other day. He said that God had something for me to do here. "

No sooner than I got those words out of my mouth, she said, "Girl, get your stuff. I think I know who you are." I picked up my stuff and lugged it across the yard to the gym.

If I live, I will never forget what happened next. I walked in the gym, and I was met by some of the meanest looking women that I had ever seen in my life. If looks could kill, I was about to drop dead right on the gym floor.

The lady who had brought me across the yard began to huddle up with the guard that was in front of the women. He kept nodding his head as she was speaking, like he was in total agreement with everything that she was saying.

Then he turned around and asked, "What is your name?"

Feeling like a little girl at her first day of kindergarten, I said, "Sonja."

He replied, "No, no we can't use your first name. What's your last name?"

I didn't know why it was so important to him, when he had all these women in front of him. But I was on strange soil, and I needed to be as agreeable as possible.

"My last name is Crutchfield," I said wondering what was next.

By this time, I noticed that there was a little twinkle in his eyes. He said, "Crutchfield, I know you know how to direct a choir."

The moment I heard choir, I thought this might not be as bad as I thought. I stood straight up and said, "Yes, sir."

Extending his hand toward the ladies on the bleachers, he said, "Choir, meet your new director, and Crutchfield, meet your new choir."

This almost sounded to me like when Jesus was dying on the cross and he said to Mary, "woman behold your son and son behold your mother."

I couldn't believe it. This was my first day in prison and I was already directing the choir.

My prison stay would be unusual to say the least. I even heard one guard say, "I don't know who she thinks she is, and why is she getting all this special treatment. She is an inmate just like everybody else."

The reality is that I never sought any special type of treatment. God just gave me favor that allowed me to do things that most inmates couldn't do. I excelled in all my responsibilities, and I was given more opportunities. I was eventually placed over a group that assisted people when they tried to commit suicide. I helped to bring in outsiders to minister to us. I even got a chance to bring in my mother's church Cherry Grove Missionary Baptist Church of Murfreesboro.

When my mother's church came, they brought about 30 people with them. For the first time in years my mother got to see me do something positive and I wasn't high while doing it. During her visit she got to see me direct the choir.

The choir was incredible! Those girls could seriously sing. As I was directing the choir, I could hear my mom shout from the back of the room, "Go ahead Candy, now that's my baby!"

For me, the choir became the turning point. I was taking the energy that I had used on crack and putting it into the choir. I didn't know it – but after I would be released, I would be allowed to take an inmate choir to churches to sing. Before I knew it, they were allowing me to take the choir to churches to sing. We would be called the Victory Voices.

There was no doubt, that I enjoyed the choir. Yet, over time I began to miss my freedom. I had done a lot of "white collar" crimes, and once I went to jail it all caught up with me. I had gotten stuck in the system. MY original 6-month sentence had turned into 3 years. No one could tell me when I was getting out.

After a while, I started asking God, "Why can't I get out of here? This doesn't make sense."

During my quest for an answer, he reminded me about the night that I was sitting by the road. He said, "You told me to keep you until you were ready to do right."

I had forgotten about that request. I knew that I was ready to do right. I couldn't give the date or the hour, but I was sure God had changed me this time.

I threw my hands up and opened my heart. I said, "Okay Lord, I am ready."

Three years and a few days in TPW, I told God that I was ready to be released. I saw a lady coming across the yard. She was carrying a lot of bags and books. She was struggling to hold on to everything. I went out to assist her. When I walked up to her, she graciously accepted my help.

As we walked in the office, I found out that she was the new internal parole officer. When meeting with her, I told her, "I think the Lord wants you to help me get out. I am stuck in here. "

With a puzzled look on her face, she asked "What are you talking about?"

I explained in detail how my 6-month sentence had turned into 3 years. I didn't know what was going on and no one would tell me.

Well, she became my third angel. She worked aggressively to get my case on the parole docket. The next thing I knew I was up for parole. I just had one small problem my rap sheet was so long that the parole office didn't believe anyone would take me. In the state of Tennessee, the only way that you can parole out of jail, is there must be a prearranged place for you to go.

For the twelve years that I had been smoking crack, I had also been burning bridges. For over a decade people had heard that I was going to change, so many times that it sounded like a broken record. Every time I went to jail, I said that I would be different when I got out. My change would only last a few months, and then I would be back into the same stuff. The last time I had gone to jail my own mother had cut me off. She wouldn't even accept any of my collect calls.

I knew that just getting out of jail was not enough. I had to find a suitable place to stay. During my prison stay I had confirmed that God was my source. Now that I needed a place to parole out to, I was going to have to trust Him to be my source.

"O come, let us sing for joy to the LORD, let us shout joyfully to the rock of our salvation." Psalm 95:1

Chapter Thirteen

Learning to Love Leonard

It was hard to believe that after 3 years, my prison stint was coming to an end. It just happened that I came up for parole at the end of the year, and this was going to be a new beginning for me.

With no one willing to take the risk of being responsible for me, my options for release were very slim. Finally, I asked the parole officer to reach out to man who I used to hang out with while I was getting high. Even when I was on drugs, he said that God told him that I was his wife. Knowing that I didn't have any other choice, I gave the parole officer Patrick's name and phone number.

When he heard that I needed a place to parole out to, I think he felt he had won the lottery. I could tell by the joyous tone of his voice that he was tickled by the fact I needed to list him as a place for me to stay. He responded with one word, "Sure."

The parole officer could not believe his response. She looked at the paper with all 32 of my previous convictions. She asked Patrick, "Are you sure that you want to take her?"

With great enthusiasm, he said "Yes, I will take Sonja Crutchfield any day. I have wanted to marry her for years. I will be more than happy to have her stay with me and my boys."

The parole officer hung up the phone and said, "Well, Crutchfield, you lucked out. It looks like you've got a place to stay."

I should have been jumping up and down, but his enthusiasm almost made me want to cringe. I knew that I didn't need any pressure for a personal relationship, but I didn't have much of a choice. I felt like Patrick was my only hope to get back into society.

After he consented to accept me, they sent someone to inspect his home. One of the guidelines for the place that you were paroling out to was that it had to be a healthy environment for you to go into. They wanted to make sure that you were not going back into a toxic situation that will route you right back to prison.

The day that I got out of jail, Patrick was waiting for me at the gate with wide open arms. The officer on duty released me into his custody. On the way to his house we made small talk, but I kept thinking what in the world have I gotten myself into. Then I had to remind myself, that I didn't have any other options. I had no other place to go, so I had to relax and be thankful that Patrick was opening his home to me. Once we got there, I let out a sigh of relief. This was a drastic change from jail. Patrick had gone out of his way to make sure that I was comfortable. He had a large 30-gallon fish tank in the living room. There was a rocking chair, and a rack full of all the current magazines, and a 50-inch big screen television in a room that was set aside just for me. Carrying my bag with the few things that I owned in it, Patrick said, "I want to make sure that you are comfortable."

I couldn't believe that he had gone through such great lengths just for me. All I could think was that he had forgotten that for the last three years I was sleeping on a hard bed in a cramped up 8-foot cell. Patrick's house was such a vast improvement that I had to stop for a moment and wrap my mind around where I was. This was almost too good to be true.

Just as I was trying to settle in, Patrick introduced me to his three sons. He and his wife had been separated for years, and he had custody of his children. They were young school-age boys, so I knew that this was going to take some adjusting. I didn't even have custody of my own children. My son was living with his grandparents, and my daughter was staying with my mother. Now Patrick was looking forward to me helping with his children.

I knew that this was going to be interesting, but I was still grateful that he had allowed me to stay with him.

My first night on the other side of bars was both exciting and scary at the same time. In 12 years, I had not been able to stay out of jail for any great length of time. Part of me was saying, "Lord, please don't let me mess up." The other part of me was wondering how in the world I had end up in such nice place.

The next day, I wanted to pinch myself because this was much more than I could have asked for. Not only did I have a very nice place to stay, but I was also getting ready to start work at a new job. I went to prison for fraud messing up people's driver's licenses and social security numbers, and now I was going to be working for the state of Tennessee fixing people's licenses at the Department of Safety.

It did not take me long to find out that Patrick was a workaholic, so he needed me about as bad as I needed him. Almost overnight I became a wife, and a mother to his kids.

This was funny because the entire time I was in prison, I had been praying that God would send me a husband. Therefore, the situation with

Patrick seemed perfect. I just needed God to confirm that he was the man that I was supposed to spend the rest of my life with.

I hadn't had sex in three years so of course, I had sex with him a couple of times. I had so much pent up sexual frustration, he seemed like the perfect outlet. I used sex to show him my gratitude for what he had done. My only dilemma was that I began to feel an internal spiritual conflict about sleeping with him, and not knowing whether he was my husband. I had started preaching while I was in prison. My moral standards had been raised, and I knew that God was not going to allow me to be "shacked up!"

One day I got a request to preach at a local church. I pulled my message together and I thought I knew what I was going to talk about. But when I got to the church, God changed my entire message. I started talking about adultery and fornication. When I began to minister, I was frozen. I could not believe that God was having me talk about what I was struggling with.

That night when I went home, I knew that things had to change. God was not going to allow me to live any kind of way and still serve him. The first thing I had to do was make sure that I clarified things with Patrick. I told him, "I know that I have kicked it with you, and you have gotten me out jail and all that kind of stuff —" I paused as I tried to pull my thoughts together. I couldn't figure out how to say it, so I just said it. With very little thought, I blurted out, "We can't have sex anymore unless we get married."

Since he was still married, I knew that we weren't going to be able to get married right away. The sex had to come to a stop.

Amid me trying to work things out with Patrick, my mother brought my daughter Montoya to stay with me. I couldn't believe that she was doing this. I was still scared that I was going to fall. When she first came to drop her off, I began to bargain with her. "Mama, I can't take care of her right now. I need some time to make sure that I am going to be okay."

After I had gotten out of jail, I had begun to see my daughter and I even started doing things to help financially for her. I just knew that I wasn't ready to step into the shoes of being her mother yet. The shoes of a mother were big to fill, and I didn't want to let my baby down anymore.

The last thing I needed for Sontoya to experience was for me to fall off the wagon, and for her to have to get on the roller coaster ride again. She was secure at my mother's house. She didn't need me upsetting everything all over again.

I guess my mother had a level of faith in me that I didn't have in myself. She knew that I wasn't going to fall again. There was something about me this time that my mama knew that I had made it.

Although I tried to come up with a million reasons why I couldn't keep Sontoya, my mother wasn't hearing any of them. With a very rigid resolve, she said, "That's your child, it isn't my child, and you are going to keep her. You are over here watching this man's children. You are going to watch your own."

Without listening to my rebuttal, Mama dropped off Sontoya and kept on going.

Having my little girl with me, only added to my pressure of finding out if Patrick was my husband. Finally, one day, I couldn't take it anymore. I cried out to God, "I need you to tell me if this man is my husband. "

A few days later it was Patrick's birthday. I knew that this would be the perfect time to get an answer from God. I sent the kids away and prepared him a romantic candle-lit dinner. I had picked a special gift to give him from the kids. I set the tone for the evening with an elegant ambiance and a level of anticipation. I knew for sure this evening that God was going to answer my question.

As I sat waiting for Patrick to take his place at the table, he walked up behind me. Placing his hands on my shoulders he said, "I know you are going to make love to me tonight, because it's my birthday."

When I heard the words, *"I know you are going to make love to me tonight,"* I got my answer. Bells and whistle went off in my head while he was uttering those words. There was no longer any doubt in my mind; I knew for sure that he was *not* my husband. God had already let me know that my husband would have to put Him first, and Patrick was letting his flesh rule him.

After that evening, I didn't want to send any mixed signals to Patrick. So as not to complicate our situation any further, I felt that it was best for me to move back in with my mother. The courts still had me listed as living with him, so I decided to still go back and forth so that I could watch after his kids. I felt like keeping his kids was the least that I could do based on the situation. I couldn't forget that he had done me a huge favor my allowing me to parole to his house.

An Unexpected Visit

One morning I stopped by to make breakfast for the kids. I still had a key to the house, and Patrick allowed me to come in and out as I pleased. As soon as I got in the house, I got busy fixing breakfast. I was tossing pans, cracking eggs and mixing up pancake batter all at the same time. Then I decided to see if Patrick was up. I walked upstairs and his bedroom door was cracked. Instead of seeing him resting, I saw another woman snuggled underneath him. I couldn't believe it; he was asking me to be his wife and he already had another woman in his bed. I had barely gotten my things out of the house. I knew that this meant this woman had to have been around before now, or he just didn't care who he slept with. Whichever the case, this only confirmed that I had made the right choice.

I guess I got the devil in me. I just slipped in the room and tapped him on the shoulder. He jumped up like he had seen a ghost. With a little mischievous spirit, I said, "Yawl breakfast is on the table downstairs."

He grabbed a towel and wrapped it around himself. He came down the stairs yelling, "Sonja this is not what you think."

"Patrick, you don't have to explain anything to me. You may have to explain something to her, but I'm good," I said. I grabbed my purse and heading toward the door.

As I shut the door to the house, I also closed the door of any possibility that I would ever be with Patrick. All I could do was thank God that He cared enough about me to allow me to see what was really going on with Patrick. I knew that God had done a new work in me, because the old Sonja would have made a big scene. Now, I had too much God in me to just go off the handle, instead, I just kept it moving. I knew that if he wasn't my husband, my husband was somewhere out there.

When I left Patrick's house that evening, I knew that God had me right where he wanted me to be. I was sitting in the palm of His hand. He had delivered me from drugs, and he had given me a commitment that was stronger than crack. More than wanting a man in my life, I wanted a genuine relationship with God.

I had been living in sin with Patrick and I could not allow anything to come between me and Jesus. I kept making my request known to God for a spouse. I didn't know any other way, but to talk to God like He was my best friend. I just kept it simple, "God, if you don't send me a husband, you know I am going to fall. "

One day I stopped by my brother's barber shop. When I walked in the door my stomach felt a little funny. It sounded like a freight train ran through it.... *chukka, chukka, chukka*. I was wondering what in the world was going on. Before I could focus on my stomach, I realized that there were a lot of people in my brother's shop. I knew I couldn't stay long. I went to the bathroom so I could figure out what was going on with my stomach. I knew that I was going to have to come back a little later.

Once I got in the bathroom, I didn't feel anything else. I just said to myself, "okay Lord, what is this?" Before I left the bathroom, I said, "Whatever it is, I am ready. "

When I went back into the shop, I could hear my brother talking to his long-time friend, Leonard. I had never met Leonard, but he and my brother have been friends for years.

As they were talking, I heard my brother say, "Man, that is my sister. You don't know my sister? She is the one that we used to pray for. She used to be on dope, but she is a preacher now."

He went on to tell him that I worked for the Department of Safety taking care of issues with driver's license.

My brother knew that Leonard had lost his driver's license, because he used to sell drugs. While he was selling drugs, the state had placed a heavy fine of over $5,000 on him. He couldn't pay it, so his license was revoked.

I think a light bulb must have gone off in my brother's head as he was telling Leonard what I did for a living. Then out of the blue he told Leonard, "Maybe she can help you get your driver's license back."

All this time Leonard seemed to be in compete shock. Shaking his head, he said, "Man, that's your sister."

Walking toward them, I again felt this churning in my stomach. This time I didn't have to wonder what it was. I knew that it was God. The spirit of God said, *"That's your husband."*

The moment those words ignited with my spirit, I lit up like a Christmas tree. I instantly began to hear words like marital boot camp. I didn't know anything about him, but all I could see was ministry.

Since I had been out of prison, I had done nothing but bug God about a husband. Now He tells me that the man I am looking at is my husband, and I began to evaluate him. I began to size Leonard up from head to toe. He didn't even look like someone that I would pick out for myself. Without even meeting him, I began to analyze the situation. Then I whispered a prayer to myself, "Lord if this is who you want for me, then let me know."

I guess I must have been looking a little dumbfounded, because my brother called me over to him and said, "I got somebody that I want you to meet." As I approached him, he said, "Sonja this is my good friend Leonard. He is a preacher and he used to pray for you when you were out in the streets."

I extended my hand and shook his, his three sons approached me, and I shook their hands as well. After shaking Leonard's hand my stomach began churning all over again. I couldn't believe that I didn't even know this guy's last name and I already was hearing wedding bells.

Right away, I knew why God had allowed me to parole out to Patrick's house. Patrick had three sons, and Leonard had three sons. I had just spent time preparing for what God had in my future.

Then out of the sky blue, my brother asked me, "Can you take Leonard home? He doesn't have his driver's license and I picked him up, but as you can see, I've gotten busy. It will be a while before I can do it. The boys are getting a little antsy too."

What else could I say but yes, I have already seen myself walking down a wedding aisle with this guy. To top it off, my brother began to brag about all the things that I was doing. He told Leonard that I was a part of the Victory Voices Choir and that I was doing speaking engagement talking about my experience in prison and how God had changed my life.

Normally this would have made me nervous, but I was very comfortable with Leonard. I wanted him to know all about me.

I think they knew that my answer was going to say yes, because Leonard said, "Give me a minute to get the boys things together."

Within moments, Leonard, the boys and I were all out the door and heading toward my car. There was a warmth that came over me as we walked toward the car. We made small talk all the way to his house. I couldn't believe that we had so much in common. He had sold drugs on the same street that I had gotten high on, yet our paths never crossed. We even knew some of the same people; his sister and I had run track together in high school, but still I had never met him. It seemed almost like God was waiting to do something in both of our lives before he brought us together.

When we pulled up to his house, I didn't want the moment to end. In a very casual manner, I reached in the glove compartment and pulled out one of my business cards. Handing it to him, I said, "I will be more than happy to look into the issue with your driver's license, just give me a call with the details."

Taking the card in his hand, he said, "Sure, and thanks so much for the ride."

He and his sons went into the house, and I thought I was going to go through the roof of my car. Who in the world was this guy? I didn't know him, but I had been "close" to him for years; our paths should have crossed.

I could not wait to get back to John's shop so that I could interrogate him about his friend. The minute that I opened the door to his barber shop, I yelled, "John, who is that guy that I just took home?"

Puzzled, John said, "What do you mean who is he? I told you that he is my friend, Leonard." I felt like a little girl. I was so excited that I could not keep still. I said, "He is my husband."

John just laughed at my comment. He said, "Sonja, you think everyone wants you. He doesn't want you. He is raising his 3 boys by himself. He is not looking for a wife."

I didn't let John's remarks faze me. I just laughed as I headed toward the door. Then I turned back and yelled, "God said Leonard's my husband!"

As I got in the car and headed home, I didn't know what was going to be next with Leonard. I knew that God had spoken, so He was going to have to work this out.

After a few weeks, God's plan began to manifest. I had started a cleaning business. My first client was a major client, Carmike Movie Theatres. And then I found out that Leonard had been laid off his job. It was a seasonal lay-off, but I figured that he could use some extra cash.

I called him up with a business proposal. When he answered the phone, I said, "John told me that you got laid off. I just got a contract for my cleaning company and I am going to need some help. Would you like to work for me?" He accepted my proposition and we instantly clicked as friends.

We were working together and spending a lot of time together. It had only been a few weeks, but it was getting harder and harder for me to keep my thoughts to myself. One day after we finished cleaning, I had him over for a bite to eat. As he was sitting there eating a big helping of my spaghetti, I said, "Now look here, I need to know if God told you anything about—"

He cut me off and became defensive. He said, "I am not your husband."

I tried to act like his response didn't faze me, but I knew that he had heard the same thing I had heard. I could have been talking about anything, but he went straight to marriage.

After that night, Leonard kept acting like our relationship wasn't fazing him. Then one of my male friends came to town and started paying attention to me. That night, we were cleaning the theater and I could tell Leonard was upset. Suddenly, he picked me up and put me on top of a trash can and said, "What do you want from me? Do you want to be my girlfriend? "

"I don't want anything. I just want to know what God is saying."

"I am telling you that he is not saying anything. I am not supposed to be your husband." It was clear that my question had bothered him

At that point, all I could do was say, "Okay." Deep inside, I knew that it was only a matter of time.

A few days later, he called me on the phone in the middle of the night. He said, "I have loved you from the day that I first saw you. God told me that you were my wife. It is just like I was running from my calling. I haven't been able to get any sleep. Will you please tell me yes so that I can get some rest?"

As much as I wanted to hear this, I couldn't believe my ears. A proposal that I had planned from the moment we met was finally happening, and I was almost speechless.

There was nothing else that I could do. I said, "Yes."

Two weeks later Leonard and I were married. I had said, yes to God, I said yes to Leonard, and I was saying yes to life. I had no idea what was going to be up the road, but I knew my journey was going to be blessed. I was walking with God, and I had the man that I loved by my side.

"Praise ye the LORD. I will praise the LORD with my whole heart, in the assembly of the upright, and in the congregation. The works of the LORD are great, sought out of all them that have pleasure therein. His work is honorable and glorious: and his righteousness endured forever. He hath made his wonderful works to be remembered: the LORD is gracious and full of compassion." Psalm 111:1-4 (KJV)

Chapter Fourteen

From Prison to Praise

My marriage to Leonard Brown only helped to solidify the call of God that was on my life. We both were preachers and many times we worked together in ministry. The more I served in ministry, the more I realized how grateful I was for all that God had done for me. He had taken me from the steel bars of a prison cell to praising him open before a congregation.

It is only fitting for me to close the end of my book with one of my sermons after I got out prison.

I was asked by my Aunt Patricia to preach the Women's Day program for Emery United Methodist Church. This was the church she attended

When the young lady introduced me to speak, she called me Candy and it reminded me of how far I had come. Candy was a very familiar name for me. My family and people in the community called me Candy. As I sat there just waiting to share the word that God had given me, the congregation was listening to her give a snapshot of my testimony. Her words only reminded me of how grateful I was for my transformation. God had taken my common name of Candy and made me walk in his chosen name for me, Sonja.

As Candy, I might rob you, write a hot check, or smoke crack. Yet, my God given name of Sonja, which means wisdom. Now, I was wise enough to know that God had much more for me than what I was doing. He didn't design for me to sleep in a dumpster, he desires for me to preach his word and set the captive free.

Looking around the church I was overwhelmed with joy. I could have been looking into a sea of inmates, but now I was staring at a congregation of believers

Once I stepped up to the pulpit, I was on fire for God. I was dressed in royal colors of purple and gold. I was ready to help people be delivered from whatever was holding them back from their destiny.

This is the message I gave on that day:

If you know the Lord say, praise the Lord. If you love the Lord, say praise the Lord. And if you know that He is always worthy of getting the highest praise, say halleluiah.

If God has blessed you to be in the house of the Lord, we are going to give honor to him. The spirit is kind of high in here, and I feel pretty good right now.

Will you bow your heads with me as I pray? Lord I just come to you as humble as I know how. Lord I am asking you to speak to me right now. Remove me, right now, so that you have room to be used by me so that someone may be touched by the word you have given me.

Please let your anointing flow through me from the top of my head to the bottom of my feet. Let me yield to the Holy Spirit right now, so that you can use me. I pray that someone is touched by the word that you have placed in me today. God whatever you have for me to give to the people, then let it be.

Thank you, Lord, for allowing me to speak. I know that I am not worthy, but I am grateful. If you didn't bless me anymore, I will be eternally be grateful for your grace and mercy.

My text today comes from Genesis 19: 4-8 (NIV).

"⁴ But before they lay down, the men of the city, even the men of Sodom, compassed the house round, both old and young, all the people from every quarter:

⁵ And they called unto Lot, and said unto him, where are the men which came into thee this night? bring them out unto us, that we may know them.

⁶ And Lot went out at the door unto them, and shut the door after him,

⁷ And said, I pray you, brethren, do not so wickedly.

⁸ Behold now, I have two daughters which have not known man; let me, I pray you, bring them out unto you, and do ye to them as is good in your eyes: only unto these men do nothing; for therefore came they under the shadow of my roof."

If I was going to give this text a title it would be, "Whatever you are pregnant with, it is time to delivery."

Now, first I like to give you the definition of pregnant. According to Webster's dictionary the definition of pregnant is the carrying of unborn offspring. Webster also defines deliver as giving birth. On the other hand, the spiritual definition of pregnant means to be full of something. The spiritual definition of delivery means the act of setting free something that hampers or holds you back. It is time to delivery.

First, let's look at the 4th verse of Genesis.

"⁴ But before they lay down, the men of the city, even the men of Sodom, compassed the house round, both old and young, all the people from every quarter.

In this verse when I think about the house around, I think about the Body of Christ. Our body is the Lord's temple. We are the house. A lot of times our lives are surrounded with sinful things like adultery, homosexuality, drug addiction, alcoholism, gossiping and lying lips.

When we allow or lives to be caught up with what the world is doing, we become pregnant with whatever those sinful issues are. If we are not prayerful, it can be easy to go down the wrong lane.

Now let's look at verse 5.

⁵ *And they called unto Lot, and said unto him, where are the men which came into thee this night? bring them out unto us, that we may know them.*

I am going to break this down a little bit for you.

This reminds me of how when people are pregnant with the wrong things, they always want you to join them in their mess. For instance, they may say: We are just going to have a little bit of fun tonight. We are not going to get too drunk like we did last night. We are just going to have one or two drinks, instead of the four of five we had last night.

Then there are those guys that are pregnant with adultery. It doesn't matter if you tell them that you are married. They will just say: What your husband doesn't know won't hurt him.

On the other hand, you have people that come to church and just sit on the bench. I call them bench warmers. They aren't involved in any organization; they don't serve on any program. They just sit on the bench. They may approach another church member to try to get them to go out to the club. They'll say: Let's go out and shake a leg for a minute. They are trying to entice you to get pregnant with the same sinful ways that they have. All the time they really need to be shaking a leg for Jesus.

Now Let's look at verse number 6.

⁶ And Lot went out at the door unto them, and shut the door after him,

This reminds me of how God stands with open arms, no matter what it is that we are doing to try to destroy ourselves. While we are busy trying to keep up with the things of the world, God desires for us to turn our lives over to Him. His arms are always waiting to welcome you back.

In closing, let's look at verses 7 & 8.

⁷ And said, I pray you, brethren, do not so wickedly.

⁸ Behold now, I have two daughters which have not known man; let me, I pray you, bring them out unto you, and do ye to them as is good in your eyes: only unto these men do nothing; for therefore came they under the shadow of my roof."

No matter what we do, the Lord stands before us giving us a better choice. We should stop seeking death and choose life. The word of God tells us to stand still and see the salvation of the Lord. We have the gift of life and death in tongue. We should be speaking life into our situation. We have people who are speaking to their children and their husbands just any kind of way. You are supposed to be representing Christ and some of you call those close to you out of their names. If you are a follower of Christ, you will start watching your tongue.

You don't have to be pregnant with sinful ways and ideas. You must remember you will deliver the fruit of whatever you are carrying. Instead of gossiping, allow God to turn you into gospel-ing. God can take you from carrying news about everyone else, to spreading His news to the world.

When I speak, I always speak to myself first? God has brought me from a mighty long way, but I still have a long way to go. There are times you might see a handsome guy and he has the bi-ceps and triceps. He is looking good and smelling good; even though he belongs to someone else you are thinking that you must have him. Then you finally get him and find out he isn't worth a quarter. You realize that you have allowed your flesh to get you off course, when you need to be concerned about the things of Christ.

You don't have to be pregnant with any of those sinful things. You can be pregnant with the Holy Ghost and deliver the anointing of God. You can be pregnant with love and give birth to warmth and affection. You can be pregnant with the word of God and give birth to kindness. You can be pregnant with self-control, and have God control your impulses and your actions. You can be pregnant with happiness and give birth to joy.

The word tells us that the joy of the Lord will be your strength. I am so glad that I have joy in my life. I can't speak for nobody else, because nobody knows Sonja like me.

When I said, nobody knows Sonja like me, something in me clicked. I realized that one night I had to cry out to get rid of the sinful things that I was pregnant with, so that I could deliver something different. I didn't want to give birth to the pain that I was carrying.

I had been hooked on crack for 12 year and had been hurting everyone that ever loved me. My life was going downhill until I took an upward direction. God took me from smoking a crack pipe to speaking about His gospel into a mic.

118

"I will extol thee, my God, O king; and I will bless thy name for ever and ever.

[2] Every day will I bless thee; and I will praise thy name for ever and ever.

[3] Great is the LORD, and greatly to be praised; and his greatness is unsearchable.

[4] One generation shall praise thy works to another and shall declare thy mighty acts.

[5] I will speak of the glorious honour of thy majesty, and of thy wondrous works.

[6] And men shall speak of the might of thy terrible acts: and I will declare thy greatness.

[7] They shall abundantly utter the memory of thy great goodness, and shall sing of thy righteousness.

[8] The LORD is gracious, and full of compassion; slow to anger, and of great mercy." **Psalm 145:1-8** (KJV)

Chapter Fifteen

Continuous Praise

There is no way I would expect you to believe that my transformation from smoking crack to being on a platform to lift the Holy Spirit has been easy. It has been an on-going process.

When I first got out of jail, I faced my first major challenge. I began to work for the Tennessee Department of Safety. My job was to assist in reinstating driver's licenses that had been suspended, revoked or cancelled. This put me in an unusual position because I went to jail for fraud and forgery.

Every day when I went to work, I had to pinch myself because I couldn't believe that I had been given such a phenomenal opportunity. On the other hand, I had to check myself because I didn't want to have a slip up and jeopardize my job.

One day when I was working, I could feel sweat rolling down my forehead. I slipped away and went to the lady's room. I fell on my knees and threw my hands up in the air. I cried out to God, "Lord, please keep me. I don't want to go down this road again."

I could feel my hands shaking, because I knew there was a voice that was trying to get me off track. All the time that I had been working, it was like this little man was sitting on my shoulders saying: *You know that you don't get high anymore. Now you got all these social security numbers and driver license at your fingertips. Just think about how much money you could make off them.*

I just wanted to scream devil, you are a liar, but my voice was silent. Something in me still wanted to listen. I needed that something to die.

While I was on the bathroom floor, I kept asking God to keep me. Before anyone realized that I was gone, I slipped back out to the floor. This wouldn't be the only time that I would have to slip away to pray. It seemed like every few days I would have to slip away and ask God to keep me. Then one day I didn't have to pray any more. The desire went away. I went to work and did my job. It no longer bothered me that I might be able to make money off the confidential information that I was given.

Winning this battle would mean that I would get another opportunity.

One day I received a call from John Price, the District Attorney who had prosecuted me on several occasions. In fact, he was the attorney who was responsible for sending me to prison. He had seen the changes that I had made in my life and wanted me to work with him part-time. He had started his own law practice and needed some help.

Answering the call to work for John Price was destiny for me. He jokingly referred to me as a frequent flyer because I was in and out of jail so much. He knew with my help; he could reach people in a few days that it would take him month to contact. I knew the streets of Murfreesboro like I knew the back of my hand.

Not only was working for Attorney Price a good business decision, it was a major spiritual move. He was the founder of an all-male choir called the Victory Voices. Since I had directed a choir in prison, he also asked me to help with his choir.

Being involved with the Victory Voices was nothing short of amazing. They didn't just sing, they performed. We would all march into to a church singing "How Great Thou Art." Then our song would be followed by a few testimonials. I would share how John Price had sent me to prison and that now we were working together. I would tell how God was using both of us to win people over for Christ. John would come up and close out the testimonial service by saying that everyone was on a docket. We all were on God's docket and just waiting for our named to be called. By the time he said that, a loud hallelujah could be heard coming from the back of the audience.

Our performances took us throughout Tennessee. We even lead revivals in Eldora, Mexico as we encouraged people to walk in victory.

Through we traveled all over spreading the good news and singing, our greatest milestone was singing at my home church, Cherry Grove Baptist Church. The Sunday we went to sing there I got chills because I had so many memories of that church when I was growing up. I knew the congregation had prayed for me over the years when I had been fighting my drug addiction.

As we were walking through the doors of the church, I recalled when I was 11 years old, I went up to the senior pastor and said," I'm going to preach at this church on day."

He had patted me on the head and said, """ Honey, little girls don't preach." At that time the church did not believe in women in ministry, and that was his way of confirming their ideology for me.

I was young but that still didn't sit well with my spirit. I always felt that if God said it, then it was settled. Now here I was walking through the doors of that church lifting the voice of God with a magnificent all male choirs. Our presence was so powerful that day that when we sang the Holy Spirit fell like never. As I was directing, I investigated the audience and I saw the faces of people who had given up on me and thought that I would never amount to anything. I began to wave my arms even harder as I pushed the choir to sing their best. By the time we finished, people were shouting and dancing down the aisles. That night some of the inmates came forth to rededicate their lives to Christ. It was amazing to see that God would give us such a tremendous victory at my home church.

This service was symbolic of the ministerial call that was on our choir. Many times, we would perform at churches where the inmates had family members. Sometimes the inmates would get out of prison and they still wanted to sing with us. In fact, one of the inmate's mother began to follow us around because she felt we helped her son turn his life around. She had given up on her son but after singing with the choir, he became one of our star members. Her son made a conscious decision to give his life to Christ, and she was grateful.

The Victory Voices gave me a sense of spiritual fulfillment. We were going back into the community and making a difference. We were showing that God's arms can reach down and save people and savage relationship. People could see that the man who had prosecuted me, came back and helped to propel me into my destiny. We began being a spearhead of hope for people

After we had been traveling around and spreading the good news through the Victory Voices for about 8 years, they rebuilt the Rutherford County Work Center. The inmates were put in pods and we weren't allowed to rehearse with more than one pod at time. Even though they were in pods before, the way the building was set up didn't allot them the manpower to bring us together for rehearsals. We tried it at first. We would rehearse with one pod on Monday, another on Tuesday, and another on Wednesday. It didn't take us long to realize that you could not have a harmonious tune if you were not all coming together at one time. With the new system in place we had to disperse Victory Voice because we were not able to bring the guys together for the rehearsals.

For the first decade of me being out of prison, my life was full of peaks and valleys. After a while God let me know that my season was over working with the Tennessee Department of Safety. I went on to work for Security Finance, a small loan company.

They taught me to do a lot of different things, and they even had me doing taxes. When they first told me that they wanted me to learn how to do taxes, I said, "Yawl aren't paying me enough money to be doing taxes. I'm not doing it." I thought they were crazy. I went home and told my husband Leonard what was going on.

That night Leonard woke up in the middle of the night. He said, "Sonja the Holy Spirit told me that you need to learn how to do taxes."

I am glad that I have always been obedient to the Holy Spirit. I calmed down and learned how to do taxes. Once 1 learned how to do taxes, I enjoyed it. Then I found out that I was getting a large bonus for doing them. I loved it even more.

After 6 years, the company reviewed my records and fired me because of my past convictions. Getting fired hurt because I tried to do things the right way. I felt treated unfair and was devastated. I hadn't hidden my background. Everyone was aware of my previous convictions. Since I was still working with John at the time, he asked me to start working with him full-time as a paralegal. John knew this was wrongful termination. He decided to sue the company for me.

What the enemy meant for evil turned out for our good. We won the lawsuit.

Winning the lawsuit gave me a feeling of victory! I decided to go into business for myself by opening my own tax office. My first discovery was in order to acquire a business license one must be fingerprinted. With over 30 convictions, I had some of the dirtiest fingerprints in Murfreesboro. When I sent in my fingerprints to get my electronic filing identification number, the lady behind the desk laughed at me. She looked at the print-out for my criminal history and said that I would never qualify to open a tax office in Murfreesboro.

I knew that I could not let her comment defeat me because I realized what God had said to me. With great confidence I told her, "The spirit of the Lord told me that I could own a tax company."

She laughed, "You better go back and talk to the Lord again because with a criminal background, you can't open a tax office."

Sure, enough when I got my letter back from the Internal Revenue Service I was denied. I wouldn't take that notice sitting down. I went to John and told him about my denial letter. I asked him would he send a letter of appeal vouching for my character. He submitted the letter and the IRS overturned the decision. I opened my tax office.

To this day, I am the proud owner of Authentic Tax Service. My office is only a few blocks away from where I had my Damascus Road experience.

Over the years I have seen God move mountains for me. It's like my mama used to say, "I am the bounce back queen". No matter what obstacle has come my way I have overcome it.

I may not have a fancy title or a degree after my name, but he gave me a B.A. I am born again.

During the peak of my drug use I had a $1,000 dollar a day drug addiction. God is so awesome. I am not on any medication nor do I smoke dope anymore. I know there is a God in heaven. The Bible tells us that when we accept Jesus Christ, we become a new creature and all old things are passed away. He forgives us for what people will never stop thinking about.

Once God cleaned me up, he allowed me to experience his divine favor. My greatest success has been all the lives that I have touched and those that I am still touching. I can give hope to those that are locked up on a regular basis. I didn't get out of my prison just for my personal praise. I try to help someone else get out of their prison so that they can find their praise.

Through it all, I give all the glory to God. I am not Candy anymore. I am somebody new. I am a living, walking testimony of what the grace of God can do. He delivered me and He can deliver you, too. God's word has taken me from prison to praise. He will set you free from whatever is holding you in bondage and you can walk in victory. For he who the son sets free is free indeed!

Sonja's Song

By Sylvia Dunnavant

God reached down and touched me in my darkest hour sitting by a curb.

An angel from heaven, allowed me to hear the sweetest voice I have ever heard.

For over 12 years, I chased something that I could never catch.

Then God stepped in and from the pits of Hell, my soul He snatched.

I went from bars of steel, to wanting to live on a street paved with gold.

I am no longer lost, for God has restored me and saved my soul.

I will shout and forever my hands will be raised.

With a joyful heart, the Lord has taken me from prison, to praise.

About the Author

Minister Sonja Brown was born in Nashville, Tennessee. Her deliverance ministry, From Prison to Praise, has carried her from London to Oklahoma as she desires to heal the broken hearted and set the captive free.

Her ministry from Prison to Praise was birthed from a 12-year drug addiction. During her mess she never lost sight of the messenger - Jesus Christ. During her drug addiction days, she would leave the crack house singing, "His Eyes are on the Sparrow." After a while she found it difficult to get high, because people no longer wanted her singing and reciting scriptures to them.

One-night Minister Sonja had a Damascus Road experience, and she cried out to God to send her to jail until she could change. After that night she went to jail for a 6-month sentence, which turned into a 3-year prison stent.

It was in prison that God broke the stronghold of crack that was over her, and she surrounded her life to Christ. She later became the Director of the Victory Voices Choir, which was a male-inmate choir that traveled to different churches to sing praises and give their testimonies.

In 2006, Minister Sonja served as an Assistant Pastor for one year at Greater First Street Baptist Church under the leadership of Pastor Norris P. Johnson in Nashville, TN. She has participated in outreach efforts as well. She's a motivational speaker, and travels throughout the country encouraging others.

Minister Sonja believes that she was delivered from drugs and living in the streets in order to help someone else become healed, delivered and set free. She lives a life devoted to assisting those who want to make a positive change in their lives.

Minister Sonja has an Associate Degree in Theology from Emmanuel Baptist College. She is a licensed, ordained minister; currently serving as Associate Minister of Cedar Grove Primitive Baptist Church in Murfreesboro, Tennessee under the leadership of the Elder Monte Lester.

She is a certified tax-preparer and owner of AuthentiQ Tax Services.

Minster Sonja has two children and resides in Tennessee.

CPSIA information can be obtained
at www.ICGtesting.com
Printed in the USA
BVHW082331150622
639856BV00008B/661